IONE

CIRCA 1930

ISBN 0-9755088-0-6

First Printing

Published By
Pend d'Oreille Press
P. O. Box 793
Ione, WA 99139
www.pendoreillepress.com

IONE

In The Nineteen Thirties

Through The Eyes Of One Of The Damn
Kids,
not everyone saw it the same way as I

For the enlightenment of those who don't
know, Ione, Washington, was a town of 500
then, that has grown to 400 now, in the far
north east corner of the state. Thirty miles
farther north and we would be punctuating
our sentences with "hey," twenty miles farther
east and we would be advertising spuds on
our license plates.

Dedicated to my Dad, Goldburn Clinton Lewis, who did the best he could for his young family, by carving out a living in a hard country at a terribly harsh time. Who died of an old man's disease at the age of 27, on Huckleberry Mountain, June 5, 1932, and was buried in an unmarked grave.

To Mickey who tolerates my sitting and ignoring her for hours on end. And to Anne Williams who saw fit to defile the pages of her baby, the Selkirk Sun, where this wisdom and wit was first published, and helped with editing and formatting, many thanks. And Donna Hambrook Bell, who never left Ione and who's brain I picked and who's photos I borrowed, Thank you.

Not to forget both the Tiger Historical Center and The Pend Oreille County Historical Society for their help with photos and research. With honorable mention to the Ione High School English teachers who instilled confidence early on by telling me I would never be a writer. Thanks, you were probably right.

FORWARD

Ione is not very old as towns go. As of this writing, (2003) other towns in the state are looking at celebrating their two hundredth anniversary while Ione is just about at its one hundredth, depending on exactly where one starts counting. In 1900, the area was only approachable by boat and settlers were few. Tiger, then known as Tiger Landing, was vying for the lead as was the town of Cement, just across Cedar Creek, now just inside the north city limits of Ione. The total population of all three would probably not have reached fifty and many of those later gave up and went back to civilization. All that remains of Cement is the hole in the rock along side the highway and a kiln chimney in the woods behind it, and Tiger is not much different. The railroad arrived about 1909, the actual beginning of the town, and the muddy track between Ione and Newport became an all weather road a few years later. My memories of the area in the thirties come from the era just twenty years after that beginning. With the railroad, several mills started up in the area with the Panhandle in Ione being the largest. A 1915 plat map of Ione shows rows of small cookie cutter houses, most of which have not survived, The Hotel Pend Oreille, which appears to have been designed to house single men, and the school. The house we are living in was built in 1911 and if the construction is typical it's understandable why more are no longer around. There's a restriction on our deed, "Any house built on this lot will be painted within one year," probably put there by a developer to preclude the building of a town of nothing but tar paper shacks. Ione owed its beginning to lumber. Lumber was king, and now the king is dead. In the late thirties as the mills disappeared the mines grew and there was an almost total change of population from the mostly older Scandinavian to younger and more diverse. Long before the end of the century, the mines also failed them and many moved to greener pastures. The town developed its gap tooth appearance as businesses followed suit, and few buildings that burned or just fell down were ever rebuilt. Over and over the town of Ione has managed to survive until the next savior appears on the scene, but just barely. At present, those persons remaining in the area are waiting with bated breath for the supposed reopening of the mines at Metaline Falls, as their salvation.

GOOD LUCK....

CHAPTER I

The house looked big. A two story clapboard that had once been white, with a full porch across the front. My grandparents house on Huckleberry Mountain. Much bigger than the place in which my folks were living in Western Washington, in the shadow of Mount Rainier. An indication of the family finances: I have a letter my mother wrote to my grandmother in 1927, when I was six months old stating she hadn't been able to get me out of gowns yet as she couldn't afford any other clothes. The time when we arrived here was the summer of 1929 when my brother Ray was about six months old.

The drive had been long, when we arrived in the families 1925 Chevrolet Coupe, from Eatonville, Washington, just east of Olympia. The we was myself at age two plus, my oldest brother at less than one year, and my parents who had become unemployed several months before, because of the depression closing the mill where my dad worked. The car was a one seat coupe with a rumble seat, into which a box had been built, meaning four people in the front as we kids weren't old enough to be trusted in back, even when it had been in it's original configuration. Besides, all the family had been able to save was in a large, round top, steamer trunk that had been fitted into the rear of the car, with two extra spares piled on top. The two mounted into the front fenders were not considered enough for such a long trip. Tires at the time were not very reliable.

The house didn't look so big on the inside, especially after everyone was inside. My mother eventually was the oldest of eight kids. Before we arrived, there were five kids plus the grandparents living at home. The house was a living room, a kitchen, and one bedroom down, and two big rooms up. There was a two hole outhouse about fifty feet out the back door, out past their attempt at a garden, and the rows of not very productive berry vines. The cow barn, with a lean-to chicken house and wood shed, was across the road from the house. Their car, a big four seat, cloth top, Hupmobile, with tall solid steel wheels and skinny high pressure tires, sat in the front yard.

Much of what follows I was to learn later. Much probably came from stories repeated by older family members when I was older. The family home, stump ranch in the language of the time, was located five miles West from Ione, off what is now Meadow Lake road. There was no Meadow lake then, it was more a swamp in a wide spot on Meadow Creek. I believe the dam that created the lake was constructed in the nineteen sixties.

The springs and swamp from which one branch of Big Muddy Creek begins were in the back yard of my grandparents place. There was no electricity, but the house was modern in one way. Running water was provided by the use of a ram. A devise that uses the power of the water, to lift water something like ten feet for each foot of drop in the water supply to the pump. One of those things I always took on faith as I didn't really understand how it could work. Water was heated by placing pipes inside the fire box of the kitchen range, and it was stored in a galvanized tank behind, or it was heated in kettles on top of the stove. This was a wood range of course, that helped to heat the house, both winter and summer. Baths were in a laundry tub on the kitchen floor, Saturday night, need it or not, and with conservation practiced by several using one change of water. The same tubs were used in following days, with the addition of a wash board, to do the laundry.

The plan was that we would stay with them until a house of our own could be secured. Securing consisted of driving around the country roads of the hill, looking at vacant houses in the area. There were several fairly close that had been abandoned by early homesteaders. Their owners, if still among the living, had long since given up trying to eke out a living on the hill so there was no worry about rental. Actually they probably had reverted to the government, as the people in many cases had not completed the improvements required for homesteaders to, "prove up," and earn title to the land. In one word, my folks would be squatters.

The road on which my grandparents house was located runs generally south from Meadow Lake road, almost exactly five miles west of Ione. When I came back I knew how to find it, because I remembered climbing up on a big rock at the intersection. When I went looking, the large rock had shrunken to only about three feet in diameter.. Many of my memories from the time had shrunk similarly.

A short mile beyond them on this road was the home of Jimmy Kinnett, and there were two other vacant houses just beyond his, but both were in bad condition. The Mac Arthur family lived approximately a half mile toward Ione on Meadow Lake, and there were two houses, long abandoned log houses, one on each side of the road, about a mile further down the hill toward town.

The Huckleberry Mountain School was on the main road, about a quarter mile up from the grandparents house. There was another house about a half mile to the north, up a road that went up the hill, from just beyond the school. This is the one my folks chose.

The house was log, originally with white chinking between the logs, but much of it was missing. It was a living room, a kitchen, and one bedroom, and had an outhouse some fifty feet behind. The outhouse was cold and down a long trail that had to be shoveled through the snow in winter, and it was hot and smelly in the summer, probably why it was located that far from the house.

The house had an attic formed by nailing boards across logs used for ceiling joists, and had packrats who made scary, scratchy, noises at night. They picked up anything, particularly anything shiny, that might be left anywhere accessible. Sometimes leaving something else in exchange. Water was hauled from almost a mile away, from Muddy Creek next to the grandparents house, in the back of the Chevrolet.

The house was cleaned where it had been inhabited by furry little things, the chinking between the logs was patched, mostly with rags and mud, and rudimentary furniture was built. Beds were made of boards over frames made from small trees, and ticks, made of straw stuffed burlap bags (Gunny bags) sewn together, were placed on top. This was our home for the next two plus years.

One memory from this house involved its ceiling. It was constructed of rough sawn boards that were green when put up and had dried and shrunk over the years, leaving cracks in between. Insulation was still a thing of the future so it was probably much warmer up in the attic than in the living area below. This fact probably led to some of the inhabitants choosing it, as they undoubtedly appreciated the warm dry place to build their nests.

My mother salvaged some boxes of old medicine bottles, from someone's enterprise of some sort, from a deserted house about half way down the hill to Ione, and made a batch of root-beer. She placed it in the attic to age. It must have been good, as it soon built up too much pressure for the bottles, old square bottles with screw on lids, and they began to explode. One would pop and jiggle the next and it would follow suit. Soon we had sticky sweet liquid dripping down from the cracks between the boards. We thought it funny, but mom cried. She knew how precious the money was that she spent for materials, in an effort to enrich the lives of her kids a bit.

CHAPTER II

Life on the mountain was never easy. It is five miles from Ione, all up hill. I walked it enough times to know, and it was a lot further back up than it ever was going down. The days we looked forward to were those when someone, a truck driver or another resident of the hill, would stop and offer a ride.

The road has been rerouted since then. At the time it came straight down the hill and crossed Little Muddy Creek on a high wooden bridge. It didn't connect to Smackout as it does now. We came out on the level below, on the road that is now known as Greenhouse Road, and we had to walk a very long half mile north before we crossed Little Muddy Creek again. I don't remember this road having a name then, for that matter I don't remember most of the road or street names that are now used throughout the area. Maybe they just didn't think signs were necessary as everyone knew where they were going back then.

I can't guarantee the veracity, but it was a much discussed story among the grown ups at the time. A log truck driver, who shall remain nameless because I can't remember his name, was hauling down the hill. He got religion. I don't know how, but he decided his hand had offended him, so he stopped his truck on the above bridge, climbed down to the water, held his hand in the cold water until it was numb, then cut it off with his pocket knife. End of story.

Ione has about four months of snow each year, but being over a thousand feet higher, we enjoyed at least two extra weeks on each end of the winter. Course I heard it said more than once, that we kids shed our shoes as soon as the snow melted enough that we could jump between the bare patches on our way to school. I still find the squishing of mud up between one's toes is a rather satisfying feeling.

When you have no electricity, this long winter is not all bad because no electricity means no refrigeration. This meant we had meat to eat longer as meats were preserved by hanging outside, and lasted as long as the cold held. In the warmer months, meat consisted of the occasional fish from the creek whenever someone got lucky, chickens that were almost all Rhode Island Reds or Barred Rocks as they were bigger, rabbits, mostly wild, and the occasional grouse or small deer, game warden permitting. Beans became the protein staple much of the time in summer.

At the grandparent's place there were several rows of very stunted berry vines along side the garden patch. There were Raspberries, Black Caps, Goose Berries, and Currants that I remember us kids sampling, but have no memory of them producing enough berries to be used for anything else.

As soon as the weather got cold enough to freeze meat hung outside, it was butchering time. Heifer calves usually survived to become milk cows and to produce more calves, but bull calves usually became steers early on and beef as soon as it became cold enough to make it possible to preserve the meat. Part of the early butchering was for the meat, but equally as important was the elimination of one animal to feed. Because of the small amount of tillable acreage on the mountain, they were not able to raise much hay. Feeding the stock through the winter was always a problem.

I'm not sure how pigs survived. I'm sure they

would have to exist on mostly table scraps, and I'm equally sure there were never many leftovers on the tables of the time. There were always pigs on every farm and butchering them was more interesting than calves. A fire was kindled under a fifty five gallon barrel of water, under a tree large enough to have a substantial limb. When the water was brought to a boil, usually a day or more on the fire, the pig was led out along side where it was killed. A rope was run from the bumper of a car, over the limb, and tied to a stick that had been pointed at both ends, and pushed through the tendons of the back legs. The pig was hoisted up into the tree and then lowered into the water for a short time, then lifted out again. This would cause the hair to loosen so it would be easy to scrape off. Usually several dips were required to eliminate most of the hair Very entertaining for us kids, but probably not for the pigs.

As soon as the ground would thaw, vegetable gardens were planted in any available ground. I can remember my mothers wrath when she woke up to find the patch she had sweat over for days had been discovered during the night by a herd of dear. What they don't eat, they are apt to pull out of the ground and destroy, and once they find the garden they will always return. Maybe that's where the term, "Jack-lighting," derives. My mother sitting out at night with a flashlight and a rifle, guarding her garden. She was mad, but I'm not sure she would have been able to shoot a deer, even if it would have been foolish enough to stick it's head inside her garden while she was there.

As I mentioned earlier, some of my recollections are from stories repeated by older people. Some of these I have trouble believing. It has been said, I spent my entire time making life interesting for my mother in one fashion or another. Not possibly me.

They tell about the time we were visiting the grandparents and I was about three. Supposedly, I climbed up on the flat roof of the chicken house and stood there screaming, afraid to move, until my mother climbed up on the roof and carried me down. I wouldn't allow anyone else to touch me. With me kicking and screaming all of the way down. Sort of like taking a cat out of a tree. I don't remember it personally, so it was probably a story dreamed up from someone's imagination, designed to embarrass me.

I also don't remember the saw on the Grandparent's front porch. The cash crop on the hill involved trees and the cutting of same. The saws were two man cross-cuts that were about eight feet long, and generally with a handle on each end. They were kept razor sharp because the Tamarack they were used on was hard as Oak. They were laid out flat on the front porch where the teeth wouldn't get damaged between uses. I managed to get my feet mixed up in one and ended with numerous cuts that bled profusely. That I vaguely remember, but am not sure why my mother became so excited.

Now we hear reports of Cougars coming right into town and attacking pets. Then was supposed to be closer to frontier life, but we kids wandered the woods from a tender age and encountered our share, Coyotes, Cougars, and Bears, but I have never heard of anyone being assaulted by any of these wild animals.

CHAPTER III

There were no jobs as such on the hill and a daily five mile commute to town with no reliable car was almost impossible. One had to provide his own employment. My granddad, L.O. True, for Loren Oscar, known as Oscar, had figured out a way to feed his own brood. He would buy property from the County for back taxes, cut the trees off, and I suspect, let it go back to the county again for back taxes. County records show the going rate at the time for a quarter section was around fifty dollars. That's one hundred sixty acres, so just over thirty cents per acre, if my math is working.

Actually he was my mothers stepfather. It was not the sort of thing that was talked about in the presence of children, but my grandmother, Effie Beulah, packed up her two kids, my mother and my Uncle Fred, my mothers brother, and moved out here from somewhere in the Chicago area of I think Canada. All I ever heard of my mystery grandfather was that he was a German Jew tailor, who sat cross-legged on a table while making clothes. And whispers about his trying to sell my mother into slavery in Chicago when she was very young. A great visual picture for a child to grow up with. It just occurred, I also don't remember ever hearing a divorce mentioned.

Another family mystery I have wondered about. My grandmother wasn't fond of her name, Effie Beulah, but she named my mother her first born, Effie Violet, and her last, Beulah Beatrice. Using both the names she didn't like on her daughters. My mother in turn went by Violet as she didn't like the Effie, but named her only girl Effie Delight. Figure. But these names were typical of the era.

My dad went to work with my grandfather. When they could find a market, they would cut logs for the mills at Ione, but much of their cutting was of cordwood. All cutting was with hand saws. Crosscuts were around eight feet long and generally had a handle on each end for use by two men. You only pull. If you push, the saw will bend and make it harder for the guy on the other end to pull it through the cut.

The favored wood for burning was old growth Tamarack as it produced more heat per cord. It was not necessarily the favorite to cut as it was like oak to saw, and the grain was usually like a corkscrew making it tough to split. Mostly, splitting was done with a series of different thickness wedges and a splitting maul, with a sharp axe to cut the splinters in the cuts. A man could put out about a cord of wood a day, and I think I remember hearing mention of six dollars a cord, delivered and stacked in Ione. It also involved a lot of walking, between home and the woods as cars weren't always reliable, and gas being available only in Ione meant they would have to make extra trips to town to keep gas in the car.

Three possible markets for the wood were the Ione school, the Ione bakery, and the Ione Laundry. The school had a huge furnace in the basement that burned four foot long cordwood. The wood was stored in a double row that was eight feet high and about a hundred feet long, across the back of the grounds. The bakery had an oven, a huge brick affair, that also used four foot long wood, burned inside the oven itself for heat. The laundry, The Ione Steam Laundry, used cord wood in their boiler to make steam for their various machines.

Many times others who lived on the hill would be involved in the operation. I was too young myself, but have a few memories of some of the people. As previously mentioned, the Mac Arthurs were the nearest neighbors. I don't remember the reason he was there, but Ronny Mac was at our house and joined us for dinner. It was common practice for some, when a new item of clothes was purchased, to just wear the new under the old clothes. Both for added warmth, and for the protection the old clothes afforded the new. Ronny reached across the table for something and my mother pointed out he had his raggedy, very dirty, shirt sleeve in the butter. He answered, "That's all right. It's already dirty anyhow," not exactly what my mother wanted to hear.

My uncle Fred, mom's oldest brother, tired of the battle to earn a living, joined the army as soon as he was old enough. It was a common practice for many youths of the era to join either the Civilian Conservation Corps, (CCCs), or the army. He was stationed at Schoefield Barracks, Honolulu, Hawaii.

My only real memory of him was the time he came home with a noisy old motor cycle. I was allowed to ride on the back of the bike as he roared around the mountain roads, and managed to get my bare heel caught in the drive chain. A lot of blood, but no permanent damage, except to my mother's nerves.

He sent my mother a grass skirt, a lei, and a Ukulele from Hawaii. Somewhere I have a picture of her posing in a waist high snow bank, on the mountain, wearing and playing them. My Uncle Frank, next in line, joined the navy a bit later as he became old enough and was assigned to a destroyer berthed in Pearl Harbor. Both uncles were there for the Japanese attack, but neither was hurt. Uncle Dick, much later, walked all the way across Europe as an Army mortar Sergeant, and all three came through the war without a scratch.

One of my earliest memories was the night I was roused by my father and told to get dressed. I was told to go down to my grandparents house and tell grandma to come as it was time. I didn't know what it was about or what it was time for, but didn't want to go. It was the night of February eighth, of 1931. This meant several feet of snow on the ground, and at night probably somewhere around zero degrees or below. Mom told me I could get one of my uncles out of bed and make him fix me some breakfast, so I finally agreed to go.

I took the kerosene lantern that was nearly as tall as me, enough so as to be awkward in the snow that was probably shoulder high, and headed down the hill. The snow was actually good as the it made getting off the trail, that had been formed by people walking, almost impossible. I was only four years old, and the noises of things moving in or snow falling off trees along the way were scary, but I knew there was a warm house and a hot breakfast ahead.

Grandpa had to pour hot water into the front of the old Hupmobile to get it started, but he took grandma, bundled up in a quilt, and they headed up the hill. My uncles didn't really want to get out of bed and fix breakfast, kept insisting it was the middle of the night, but I persisted in telling him my mother said he had to until I won. When I got home the next night, I had a new brother.

This was a bad weather year on the hill. Jimmy Kinette, an older man who lived about half a mile down the road beyond my grandparents house, didn't come around for a few days so someone went to check on him. It appeared he had succumbed to a heart attack, but no one was sure . They also didn't know for certain how long he had been dead as the fire in the wood stove had burned out and he was frozen solid. Another vivid picture for us kids to discus. My dad said he hoped he would go as quickly and painlessly when it was his turn.

CHAPTER IV

Along about the fall of 1931, with three kids, my dad decided we needed a new larger house. He went about three miles further up Meadow Lake Road and started to build a house on a piece of property that my grandfather had purchased. It was just up the hill from what is now Meadow Lake Park. He would take his lunch in a brown paper sack and head out early in the morning, of days he didn't have to work in the woods. He would come home in the evening, sometimes well after dark. The same kind of hours the men put in when they were working in the woods.

The house he was building was to be two stories, part logs, with split cedar shakes on the outside of the upper part as well as the roof. It was tall and narrow, probably three rooms on the ground floor and two up. I remember it sitting there with no glass in the windows, so it left the impression of blind eyes staring out at you. This house is now the pile of logs covered by berry vines, beside the shelter cabin the forest service has built along the Meadow Creek road, just above Big Meadow Lake. It has a sign on it that states it is an example of how the pioneers built their houses. I categorically deny being old enough to be called a pioneer.

It was the evening of June sixth of 1932 that I made my second trip down the hill to my grandparents house, in the dark. There was no snow and I was older, over five, so my lantern didn't drag, but it was a lot easier to loose the trail. There were a lot more noises coming out of the woods also as more animals were astir. My dad had been working on the house. My mother was alone with us three boys, the youngest just over one year old.

We were all waiting for him to come home so we could eat dinner. At first mom said he would be home before dark because dark came late in June, then she changed it to maybe he worked until dark and then had to walk the three miles home, but it was plain she was getting worried. Finally she gave me the lantern and told me to go down and tell my grandparents he hadn't come home.

My grandparents and my uncle loaded into the car and headed up the hill. They were gone a long time and then only my grandpa and my uncle came back, and they brought my brother Ray with them. They said grandma was staying with mom and the baby. There was a lot of low talking and then Grandpa said he had to go to town and we were to stay there for the night.

The next morning when I went home, I could tell my mom had been crying as her eyes were all red. My Grandma was still with her, but my dad still wasn't there. Over the next few days there were many people in and out and a lot of crying, and talk we kids weren't supposed to hear. Nobody would answer when I asked them where my dad was.

My other Grandma came from Rainier. The one with the pointed nose and the funny hat, in her Studebaker with the long nose and extra little seats in back. I liked the car, but she didn't really look like a grandma. Grandmas are supposed to look happy, not like their faces hurt. They said they had to go to something called a funeral where kids couldn't go. We had to stay at Grandma's house with some of the older kids until they got back. My dad wasn't there either.

When they came back, there was a big argument

between my mom and my other Grandma. She said she was going to take me with her, back to Eatonville, because my mom wouldn't be able to take care of three kids by herself. Mom told her to get in her fancy car and leave. The grandma threatened to get the sheriff, and said he would make me go with her. Mom told her that she would get her rifle and shoot her if she didn't leave. She finally left, and I have never seen her in the seventy odd years since.

It was much later that I heard, my dad got his earlier wish, just much sooner than he would have chosen. They said he sat down with his back against the front of the house to eat his lunch and had a sudden heart attack. He hadn't even finished eating his lunch. By the time I heard, there were few details, but they always said he died of an old mans disease, at the age of twenty seven.

That summer, my granddad and uncles built a small new house next to my grandparents house for my mother and us kids. It was built with shiplap lumber so you didn't have to be careful about knocking out the chinking and we didn't have packrats in the attic anymore. It was also more fun living there because we were close to my aunts and uncles, so there was more to do. We kids wandered the woods all of the time, with no one worrying about our getting lost, even before we were old enough to attend school.

We did some things that would not be approved today. For that matter they probably wouldn't have met with too much approval at the time if my mom had known about them.

One such. Someone, I don't remember who, had an old single barrel, eight gauge shotgun. We used to sneak it out and shoot at gophers with it. Probably should say in the general direction of gophers. It was so heavy we could hardly lift it, and when it fired it would knock most of us off our feet. Our solution was to back up to a fence post with the stock under our arm and brace the butt against the post to absorb the kick. This made it difficult to get a good look down the sights. Gopher mortality probably wasn't too high.

We went over to Jimmy Kinnett's old house. Actually we gave the house a wide berth, remembering the stories of his death, but there was a neat old car in a pole barn out behind. Pole barns then were barns built with skinny poles stacked like log houses except with wider cracks between the poles, and generally with split cedar shake roofs. The only thing solid was the roof. The car was up on blocks and like new. A bright red Ford with black fenders and lots of brass fittings, a brass radiator frame, and carbide lamps on each front fender. Be worth a fortune to collectors today, but not worth moving at the time.

We also did a lot of harmless kid stuff. Like catching the kind of Bumble Bees that don't have a stinger, in glass jars. Mistakes were a good learning experience as the ones with stingers looked almost the same.

Then there were Doodle bugs. I'm still not sure they were not a trick, sort of like snipe hunting, that older kids played on the younger. The bugs were real. They make inverted cones, like dimples, as they corkscrew themselves backward into the dirt, most often in the dust that collects in the center of dirt roads. The idea was to bend close and repeat endlessly; Doodle, Doodle, Doodle, Doodle, until the bug would crawl back out. Maybe from boredom. At least that is what we were told. I doodled a lot, but don't remember any bugs ever backing out.

CHAPTER V

Life on the hill was good for us kids. We didn't know of all of the problems the family was having to surmount to keep everyone fed. Days in warmer weather were mostly spent in the woods where it wasn't hard to find something to do, not always on the approved list, but meeting our idea of entertainment.

Technology was beginning to catch up. We spent many hours in the evening listening to the scratchy offerings of the Atwater Kent radio that my Grandparents had set up in their living room. People today would laugh, I am sure it was limited too one or two stations, but to us it was a marvel. It must not have carried any memorable programs as I have no memories of any of them, but I do remember the setup.

It was somewhat like the modern component sound setups of today. The radio, in it's square metal box, sat on a shelf, with a six volt car battery on the shelf underneath. A one volt dry cell sat beside it. Another dry cell battery of about forty volts, a wooden box filled by a number of cells about the size of today's AA batteries, wired in series, was also beside it . They were referred to as A, B, and C, batteries. One had to be careful not to run too long on the car battery before reinstalling it in the car or it would no longer start the car. Hand cranking was avoided if possible as the car engines were large, most six or eight cylinders in line, and even though low compression, hard to turn over and usually not too eager to fire.

Another memory is the time the grandparents went

to visit family in the Lewiston, Idaho, area. They stopped somewhere, probably Spokane, and came back talking about seeing a talkie. We kids didn't even know what a movie was, silent or talking. There was a movie house in Ione, but that was much farther than we ever traveled at night, and cost more than was ever available. Much later I found out the tickets were a quarter each, a sizeable amount for several kids, when a man's wages were in the dollar per day range.

While they were gone we kids stayed on the hill, with the older ones as baby sitters. Someone came up with the idea of making taffy. It was probably not cooked long enough as somehow, no matter how long we worked it, it didn't ever get hard. Just stayed in sticky gobs. The family had a big yellow hound dog, Murphy was his name I think. Don't know who's idea it was, but he was thrown a ball of the sticky stuff. He entertained us all afternoon with it. It was too sticky to swallow, but would stick his jaws together so he couldn't get his mouth open to get it out of his mouth. He would roll around on the porch trying to paw it out, but it was too good to not eat. He would pick it up and try again, endlessly, until he finally was able to swallow it. No point to the story, just a memory. Probably get us arrested for animal abuse today.

I heard later that these visited relatives lived in Idaho, up the Salmon river on a ranch, probably another stump ranch not too different from our Huckleberry hill place, where they had to ride a hand car suspended from a cable, across the river to get home.

The reason for the trip was for the funeral of a cousin, about my age, who was kicked in the stomach by a horse. He died, because of the isolation. They were unable to get him out to take him to a hospital or get a doctor in to the ranch in time to save his life.

I'm not sure if it was before or after this trip that the Idaho branch of the family sent us a wild turkey they had shot, for our Thanksgiving dinner. It was shipped by Greyhound bus, the UPS of the day. It was cold enough in Idaho that the bird was frozen when it started, and on the bus it would have been placed in the baggage area underneath where it was also cold., But some well meaning person along the way stored it inside of a bus station when it had to stay over night. When it arrived at Ione, it was thawed, but would probably have been all right except for the giblets that were stored inside. They had spoiled and the whole bird smelled bad so it was thrown away. Thanksgiving probably was not a good day for one of the roosters, because he became the substitute for the turkey on the dinner table.

My mother at twenty six years old was a good looking woman. She had several local men willing to help her forget her sorrows, but serious suitors for a woman with three kids weren't so numerous. She had her problems in areas where she had been able to rely on male help in the past. One thing she had a problem with was shooting a deer. Venison was always handy on the hill and considered a staple by most, and she was ready to cook it, but she just couldn't bring herself to shoot one of the cute little things. Guess she had forgotten her earlier feud with them over her garden.

Another similar happening was the time she wanted to make a dinner out of a rooster who wandered the yard. She pursued him with an axe, but couldn't catch him. Then she put down the axe and lured him with feed. After she finally caught him she couldn't bring herself the apply the axe. She was quite good with a rifle, so she turned him loose and brought out the 22. She aimed for his head, but missed slightly. She hit the birds neck. The head dropped, but the rooster didn't. He went running off into the woods with his head hanging down between his legs. Mom decided to have something besides chicken for dinner. When Grandpa came home he found the rooster and finished the slaying, but mom told him to keep the chicken, she didn't have the heart, or maybe stomach, to eat him.

Another example was the time she borrowed Grampa's Hupmobile. As I mentioned before, it had large solid steel wheels and skinny high pressure tires. The tires had a habit of going flat on a irregular but often basis. Mom managed to get it jacked up and the bad wheel off, but had a problem with lifting the spare off the rear of the car where it was mounted. She had heard the tires had forty pounds of air in them, so she decided it would be forty pounds lighter without the air and she would be able to lift it easier. So she let the air out. Took her a while to live that one down.

That fall of 1932, at the age of five, I started school at Huckleberry Mountain school. Mrs. Kirkland was the teacher and she had nine students. There were four Trues: Frank, Dick, Dora, and Betty. All were my aunts and uncles. Four MacArthurs; Ronnie, Twins Phil and Bill, and Gracie. And me. I think I was the youngest, but not by much, as my aunt Betty was only nine days older than I.

There is a photo of this class on the wall of the Cutter Theater Museum at Metaline Falls, titled a photo of a historical school on Huckleberry Mountain. I'm the one in the middle down front. Not sure I totally approve. I keep showing up in things they call historical and I'm not yet ready to admit that I am history.

The school was one room with a about a dozen desks, a large pot belly stove that the older boys kept fed in the cold months, and a rack across the wall behind the stove, above the wood pile, for wet clothes. Probably mostly snowy clothes from snowball fights until they warmed. It always smelled like wet clothes. The outhouse out behind the school had separate accommodations for boys and girls and also smelled, but not of wet clothes, especially in warm weather.

At five years of age, I probably would not have been able to start at a larger school. I am convinced that partly because in the small school, where the several grades in were one room, and the younger students were able to see what their older siblings were studying, they picked things up more quickly than they would have otherwise. I never had any problems, except boredom, in any of the schools I later attended, in spite of the fact I was always the youngest boy in the class. Later, at Ione, Zelva Boyer split the title with me. She was about a month younger than I and the youngest girl, and also the youngest student throughout the ten years I spent there.

All that remains of the Huckleberry Mountain School is a few bricks from the chimney and a mushroom shaped piece of cement that was the anchor for the flag pole that stood out in front. I have heard the school was moved to Ione where it became a home, and is located on the south west corner of 7th and Houghton.

A frequent visitor and dinner guest during this

year was Ole Alldredge, a log truck driver who was from Kettle Falls originally. His sister was postmaster in Kettle for many years. He was around for some time until one day he and mom went to Colville and came home and announced that they were married. Nothing much changed until the end of the school year, but then we moved into Ione. Ole was hauling lumber for Clarence Reed's mill and it would be more convenient. The mill was I believe, on the road that goes west from the cemetery, what is now Youngren road. All that remains of the mill is a small weed grown pond, that used to be larger, where the logs were dumped. I think the fallen down house that is on the east side of the pond is where the Weaver family lived.

We first lived in a small, what was called a, 'shotgun,' house on the corner of what is now Chippewa and Mc Innis. The streets didn't have names then that I am aware of, but I was to learn this was the wrong side of the dam. To the town kids, we were the damn kids, analogous to across the tracks elsewhere. Notice the "N" added. Even though it is dirt fill and is what holds back the two Muddy Creeks to form the mill pond, I haven't heard anyone refer to it as the dam lately. It's now commonly called bridge.

A shotgun house I believe was so called, because the doors were lined up so if they were open, one could shoot through the front door and out the back without hitting a wall. This one was a living room, a bed room, and a kitchen, all in a row, with an outhouse out behind. For us it became two bedrooms and a kitchen, living room, dining room, combination that doubled for a bath room with the addition of a wash tub on the floor on Saturday night.

Ole, I am not sure why but we never called our

step dad anything else in about forty years, even though he invested his whole life in supporting us, was hauling lumber for the Reed mill at the time, usually to the farm country south of Spokane. His truck, a late 20's or early 30's Chevrolet, was parked in the yard whenever he was in town.

There was a board fence across the back of the lot to the south, and a large barn in the area behind it where we kept a couple of cows. Cows can be the dumbest and orneriest things alive when they decide to work at it. We had one who considered a fence a personal challenge and would manage to break out no matter what we did. Much of the time she wore a yoke fashioned from the crotch of a tree that was clamped around her neck to keep her from going through a barbwire fence, but it wasn't very effective on her because of her persistence. More often than not she would just walk on through and head directly for the river bank as soon as she escaped.

On one occasion, Ole was trying to lead her back through the hole in the board fence where she had knocked off a board to escape. She dug in and refused to go back through the hole she had created on her way out, so he told me to get behind and twist her tail. I did so and suddenly was standing there holding about a foot of the end of her tail, that was no longer attached to the cow. Ole then explained to me that he meant I was to twist up near the top where it would cause her some discomfort, but not as much as I had accomplished. She did go through the fence though.

CHAPTER VI

I have many memories of life in Ione, but have trouble with the time frame in the early years. The house on Chippewa was only home for a couple of years. All told, I lived in three houses in Ione and two on the mountain. And every one of them has been torn down. Somebody trying to tell me something, maybe?

On the rise across McInnis from our first house, was a small white house with what we considered a strange little old lady. She was a Seventh Day Adventist and even though we didn't know what that meant we knew we were to respect it. We were warned she was not to be bothered on Saturday, which wasn't a handicap as she locked herself in the house and we never saw her from Friday evening until Sunday.

To the north of her was an open field with merely tire tracks up around the back of the next house to the north where my friend, Raymond Swanner lived. I remember his house being on a fairly high hill, and remember his little brother riding down the hill on a bicycle he was too small to control, ramming a telephone pole, and doing serious damage to tender parts of the male anatomy, on the bolt that held the handle bars. He had to go to the local hospital for Doc Canning to patch him up. Being typical boys, we made his life miserable with such questions, as whether they used fancy embroidery stitches in the repair job. The hill is no longer there, or at least it certainly is not as high as I remember it, and would create no problems for a bicyclist of most any age.

The area behind the houses was wooded and only trails led down toward the river. There was an old road, just two tire marks really, that went along the top of the river bank south to the bridge. Garbage had been dumped over the bank in numerous places along this road. There were many Hazel Nut and Elder Berry bushes among the trees, that we kept harvested in season. Elder berries were only good for flavoring apple jelly as there was nothing to them but seed and a little juice, and this wasn't very sweet.

I remember being out behind the Adventist ladies house one bright moonlight night and watching a mother skunk lead her brood across the clearing. She led off and four babies followed, white striped tails high, single file and all in a row. I wondered if they were on their way back from raiding the ladies chicken house. This area has all been cleared and has several houses and a fire house on it now. Again I'm not sure what happened to the hill I remember being there.

On the corner of Wisconsin and the highway was a service station. I believe it was a Signal station. Several other businesses have occupied the space since, most recently a Laundromat. Regular was twenty five cents a gallon, and dispensed by hand pumps that were round and about seven feet tall. The gas was pumped from the underground tank by a long handle on the side of the pump, up into a glass bowl on top of the pump. The bowl was marked in gallons on it's sides, holding up to ten gallons. More than ten gallons meant filling the bowl two or more times, but two fifty was probably all most could afford at one time anyway. From there the gas was drained into the car tank by gravity.

On the northeast corner across the highway, was

and still is, a large apple tree. During the apple season, which fortunately happens about the same time school begins for the year, all of the kids who lived in the area enjoyed the fruit on their way home. The fence beside it had a two by six laid flat for a top, and the best fruit could only be reached when standing on top of it.

One day, I picked several apples and took them home with me. Ole (step dad) asked where I got them and wouldn't believe the people didn't object. He went with me and made me knock on their door and give the woman the apples, and apologize for stealing them. I can still see the woman standing in her doorway with a bewildered look on her face, with the apples in hand, as we walked away. It was a different time.

The apple tree is still there and still has lots of fruit, but the apples don't look as large or as succulent as I remember. The two by six on the fence is gone, as is the woman and the house where the woman lived. The house has been replaced by a characterless single wide. Also gone is the house down the street to the east where another friend Leonard Johnson lived. I remember spending hours in his yard fixing bicycles. This is where we invented the playing cards clipped by clothespins to the bike frame, so they hit in the spokes to make motor sounds for the bikes. Or at least we thought we invented it.

Kids today are deprived of the opportunities to develop their imaginations that we had. They are stuck with all these electronics that do their thinking for them when they push the buttons. We were blessed with inner tubes that were made of real rubber which we used for lots of our inventions, sling shots being the most common. We made guns that shot rubber bands about half an inch wide cut from the tubes. First came pistols with one clothespin on the back for a trigger and fired one rubber band. They evolved into repeaters as more clothespins were added on the sides or any other place we could find room. Sometimes as many as six, and sometimes only until the mother who unwittingly furnished them found where they had disappeared to.

Rifles whittled out of boards came next as they stretched the rubber more and would shoot farther. Then someone figured out if the board was tongue and groove, and carved with the groove up, an arrow would fit in the slot and could be shot from it. Arrows were made from a shingle with the thin end passing for feathers and a rifle shell on the other end for a weighted point. Fitted into the slot, the rubber would fire the arrow about a city block. Sometimes at a live target, like maybe another kid. As I said, a lot more educational than playing with a couple buttons.

The Oscarson family lived in a yellow and white house on, I think, the north west corner of this intersection where there is a garage today. They had twelve kids and we heard it said, they were shooting for eighteen. We also heard that the family acted sort of militarily. Age equated to rank. The older supervised the younger, and kids graduated from high school into assisting in supporting the rest of the family. Odd to us, but we figured it must be the Nordic heritage. Ralph was my age, but Doris was much cuter, and I lost some good friends in the late thirties when the mill closed and their family was one of those who moved away.

Perhaps the hardest thing to get used to was moving from a one room school into the Ione School.

It now bears a historical building sign designating it as Ione High School and in one historic reference I have seen it labeled Selkirk High. Actually it was just the Ione School and one was required to work his way up to high school on the third floor.

Entering the front door, you encountered a wide stair going up and a narrower stair on each side going down. On the right in the half basement was the first grade room in the front and the girls bathroom in the back. Down the left side was the second grade room in front and the boys bathroom in the rear. Between the two rest rooms on the back was the furnace room, with a huge furnace that burned four foot long cord wood to heat water into steam to power the radiators in the various rooms. There was a fuel supply, a double stack of cord wood about eight feet high, all the way across the back of the school grounds.

Second graders graduated up the wide stairway to the second floor, where the third, fourth, and fifth grades shared the two front rooms. The sixth, seventh, and eighth grades shared the two rooms in the rear. The office was in the space opposite the stairs and between the sixth to eighth grade rooms, over the furnace room. The west end of the hallway, about the size of an average sized bedroom in a house, housed the grade school library.

After eight long years the student was deemed ready for high school and the heights of the top floor. The front room on the right was the science lab. On the left front was the social studies and math room. Algebra was taught one year and geometry the next, with trig thrown in periodically. The lucky ones were the ones who started high school on the year that allowed them to get the subjects in the proper sequence. I wasn't lucky.

The small room on the north west corner was the English room, only large enough for about a dozen students. The large room in the center on the north was the study hall where every student had a desk. At the time I got there, there were a number of vacant desks, and by the time I left, there were a lot more. This room was looked over by a photo of the County Superintendent of Schools, a rather sour looking lady, and another of President Roosevelt, from the front wall. The small room in the north east corner, no larger than the English room was the high school library.

CHAPTER VII

We wandered around the Ione area much as we had on the mountain, but our range was fairly limited compared to today. Tiger was another world, as were the Metalines. On foot, we were mainly limited to the area from the cemetery on the south to the town dump, about half mile north of town. We spent a lot of time at the dump because it had many fascinating items, that had a habit of following us home despite continual attempts at parental guidance.

It was possible to find most anything there. More than one car was driven or dragged to it and pushed over the river bank. Some items stopped on the side of the hill, at least until we supplied another push, and some just ran down and floated down the river. Our range on the river bank was probably slightly longer on each end than it was above.

As I mentioned earlier, my step dad was hauling lumber to the Spokane area. I made the trip with him a few times. We would climb into the previously loaded truck before full daylight with our brown bag lunch and head out south. The truck was hot and noisy, and smelled of hot oil and exhaust, but for me it was the height of adventure. Everything beyond Tiger junction was all new to me because our trips usually involved turning west to Colville. At forty or forty-five miles per hour, there was lots of time for looking. Still more time when the truck would have to grind up the hills in a lower gear.

The places reel off slowly; Blue Slide, with its cabins and store, most of which is still there, but showing its age. Ruby, a small store and gas station, there is no sign of it now. Locke, the same, has also disappeared, and the highway has moved away from its site.

All I remember of Cusick from this trip was the bleachers of the rodeo grounds, and some Indians riding horses along side the road. Ione hadn't been blessed. To my knowledge there were no members of any minority, except the Japanese Teroka family who operated the Ione Laundry, in the town or going to the school in all of my time there.

Out of boredom, I dug the shipping documents out and figured, my inclination now is to say computed, but that would have been a science fiction idea then, how much the lumber on the truck was worth. This was a full size truck with a short trailer behind. The whole load was costing someone over three hundred dollars. A small fortune in my life at the time. Considerably less than what a partial load on a small pickup would cost today.

After Cusick was Usk, and Jared, both of which almost don't exist. Newport like Ione hasn't changed much. Closer to Spokane, the towns that have now grown to their own cities, were just convenience stores on the highway. Riverside was slightly bigger, as was Hillyard, since totally devoured by Spokane.

We went through Spokane, right down Division through the center of town as is now necessary, except there was much less town. Sprague and Boone remain in my memory for some unknown reason. We continued on south through Ritzville to a farm south of town where they were building a large barn. I watched as Ole cranked some rollers under the load until it began to teeter, then jumped the truck a couple times until the lumber unloaded itself.

After loading the trailer on to the back of the

truck, we parked in the shade of a tree and ate the lunch we had carried. Peanut butter on a slab of homemade bread, with a piece of cake for desert, tasted good as it'd been a long time since breakfast. Ole had coffee, but I hadn't yet acquired the taste so there was ample water from a hand pump to drink. It tasted funny, not like Cedar Creek water, so I didn't drink very much. We retraced our route and arrived back home late in the afternoon. On these trips, I usually crapped out and slept the last few miles.

I wasn't along on one of his trips when he came back with the truck all messed up on the right side. He had run over a pig. He said, "If you hit a bear or a pig it is just like running over a big rock. There is no give to them. All you can do is just bail out and let the truck go." He had just opened the door and stepped out, and then righted the truck, checked the oil, and drove it home.

After about two years we moved to a house south off Sullivan Lake road. The present McInnis street became our driveway when it crossed Sullivan Lake Road. It was a two story house that I considered a large house after the one we had been living in, at the end of what I only considered a long driveway in the winter when I got to shovel the snow off it. The house faced west towards the highway with a large open field and a pond between it and the roadway.

The highway was tarred, but different from today's blacktop. At some point the road people were resurfacing it and we kids discovered, if the tar they were applying was allowed to cool, it could be chewed like gum. Not much taste, but the price was right in line with our finances.

The new house had a kitchen, a living room, and one bedroom down, with a stairs up the middle separating the upstairs into two open areas where there was no inside finish. We could lay in bed and look at the inside of the siding and the two by fours of the framework.

It had a screened in back porch add on, and a root cellar underneath where things stayed fairly cool in summer. Water came from a hand pump mounted on the kitchen drain board. One had to remember to save enough water to prime the pump the next time it was to be used or it wouldn't produce any water.

Bathing was still in a wash tub in the kitchen, in water heated on the wood range. In the summer, mom sometimes allowed swimming to replace the Saturday night ritual. Probably in part because the heating of water with a wood stove did a lot of heating of the house at the same time.

Behind the house there was a woodshed with a crude carport, made of peeled poles with a shake roof, attached to its side. This was the residence of the family car, a 1927 Chevrolet four door sedan. The back doors opened forward, so were called suicide doors. On the other end of the woodshed was the outhouse.

About a hundred feet south beyond the house was a rough cow barn with a pigpen on one end and a lean-to for chickens on the other. Midway between the pigpen and the house was a large yellow pine tree where it was convenient for butchering, and in cold weather it was usually decorated with frozen meat hanging up high enough to escape the meat eating wild animals, from the limbs on ropes that allowed it to be lowered for parts to be cut off.

I have a few more memories of this house as we lived here longer and I was somewhat older by the time we moved. Some good, some not so good. We had a Philco magic eye radio for entertainment, a big improvement over the Atwater Kent of Huckleberry Mountain, made possible because we had electricity. It had a green eye that glowed brighter as you tuned in a station. An AM station that is as FM had not been thought of yet. We spent a lot of time in front of it. Staples like Fibber Mcgee and Molly and Jack Benny, and always a favorite for us kids, The Shadow Knows. But we still had no refrigeration, and water was not piped as it had been on the mountain, and still had to be heated on the top of the wood stove.

I remember coming down stairs one evening and finding my mother sitting in the living room, wreathed in smoke, and trying to hide a cigarette. She finally explained that she was trying to learn to smoke. She must have been successful as she smoked as long as she lived, another fifty odd years at least. As a contrast, Ole also smoked, but told us several times that if he caught any of us smoking, he would load up his pipe and make us sit in front of him and smoke it, hinting that it would probably make us sick. "Because smoking caused cancer." That was seventy years ago, but today it is fashionable to blame the cigarette companies for cancers caused by people who had no idea cigarettes would do that. Don't think he ever tumbled to the fact that we snuck his pipe out and smoked leaves or Indian Tobacco in it on many occasions.

We were bothered by yellow jackets in the summer because the house was single wall construction and they could come and go as they pleased under the eaves. More than once we went to bed and got stung on our feet by bees who had crawled down under the covers on the bed. Not sure what the attraction could have been, but possibilities are endless as we went barefoot all summer and I'm sure weren't always diligent in washing our feet before bedtime.

The man in the house across the highway built a moving target in his yard for bird hunting practice. He strung a cable up to the top of a tree, with a fake duck hanging on a pulley, with an arrangement that would cause it to run quickly up the cable. It could then be pulled back down for another trip. The men would stand behind it and shoot at it with shotguns. In winter when the snow had a crust on it us kids would stand out in our yard and collect the pellets as they fell on to the white surface. In summer it was impossible to find them. Today someone would certainly call the Sheriff.

There was nothing between our house and the river and its bridge except woods. Now several houses are there, and Dawson Construction is in what used to be our Alfalfa field. An incident I recall that involved the Alfalfa field was the time one of the cows got into it. As I have stated, they were so cantankerous a fence was just a challenge. This time, she forced her way in rather than out, and gorged herself on green Alfalfa which is a definite no-no. She puffed up like someone had used a tire pump. Ole's solution was to take his jackknife and stick it into her side, between her ribs. It was like he had punctured a tire, except the smell was definitely not that of a tire. The cow did get better.

There were lots of Hazel nuts in the woods of the area, but they were so plentiful that there was no market for them and we weren't able to sell them. We did eat a lot of them though as we usually couldn't afford any other sort of nuts and they did flavor moms desserts.

One day we encountered a skunk in our private woods. Skunks were usually eliminated as soon as possible as they could wreak havoc in the hen house. He ran into a clump of brush and we threw rocks at him. Rocks were in short supply, so we were soon posted on three sides of the bushes where we could catch rocks thrown by the guy on the other side as they bounced out, and throw them back at the skunk from our side. We ultimately got the skunk, but not before he got us. Indirectly. He sprayed the brush and as the rock would go through it would get wet so when we reused it we would get wet. We were not very socially acceptable for the next week or so afterwards. Must have been summer time as I don't recall any impromptu vacations from school and I'm sure we would have been excused.

CHAPTER VIII

By the early 1930s Ione owed its existence to the Panhandle Lumber Company mill. There were several mills constructed along the railroad North of Newport after it was built in the early years of the century, but the Ione mill was the largest. Many of the smaller houses in the town look to be from the same plans and my guess is they were originally mill houses. The Coyner building on the corner of Central and Main was originally The Hotel Pend Oreille, and was merely sleeping rooms, with one bath on each floor and a restaurant on the ground floor. Just right for bachelor mill workers.

If you have ever wondered why the town ends so abruptly at the alley on the south end of town, the mill was responsible for that also. The lumber yard used to fill this space with enough lumber to build several Iones. There were narrow gauge rail lines through the area and lumber was hand stacked to probably fifteen feet high over the whole area from the present alley south of Blackwell to the mill. Probably at least three normal city blocks.

Stackers couldn't smoke because of the fire hazard so they chewed Beechnut Chewing tobacco and cached their supply in the stacks. We kids, really weren't supposed to be there at all, but we used to find it and learned, sometimes the hard way, that though it tasted sweet we should not swallow the juice.

I remember the mill as a very large, red, wood frame building, spread along the west side of the mill pond, with a very tall, red brick smoke stack at its north end. This stack outlived the mill by several years, not coming down until sometime after WW2.

Most of the people in the area either worked in the mill or in the woods cutting timber to feed it. It also did some things for the community that were not so well known. Some of them not even to those who ran the mill. We kids were able to create or adapt some of them to our own use.

The mill furnished electricity for the town. The building on the corner of Central and Houghton, recently vacated by the library and now housing part of the Town Offices, was the Water and Light office. I don't know if that would indicate the mill was responsible for the water that came from a dam up Cedar Creek also, but regardless, we had no interest in the water part.

The railroad used to arrive at the mill on a trestle that is still visible as a few pilings at the west corner of the pond where Muddy Creek enters. We fished off the trestle and swam off it during the summer. In winter we skated around it and also swam under it. That's not an error, we swam under it all winter. The mill burned wood to create steam to make electricity for the town as well as the mill. The turbine outflow was into the pond under where the trestle ended at the bank, at the south end of the mill. It was a pipe of about twelve inches, and the water was just slightly hotter than what would be comfortable to sit under. It kept the ice thawed in a circle of about a hundred feet across. Near the pipe the water was like bath water, but the warm got shallower the further out one went. Out near the edge of the ice the warm got so thin that anything hanging down was almost frozen. Skinny dipping was the usual.

The time between the warm water and getting clothed again in the frigid air was kept as short as possible. A favorite trick of some of the older kids was to grab the clothes of someone smaller and soak them so they would freeze while he was swimming or almost freeze before he could get into them and get home.

The pond was meant for storing and delivering logs to the mill. Logs came into it by rail, by truck, and also by water via the river. There is almost no sign of it now, but early on the river probably delivered more than the others.

There was a boom running up the middle of the river from the center of the dam, almost a mile, to the bridge. It was anchored by a string of pilings, a few of which remain and were in the news recently as a danger to boaters. The boom was designed to catch logs that were free-floated down the river from where they were cut and or dumped, from both sides of the river. This would have made it possible to catch logs from all of the way up to Newport. They were swept to the west side of the river and behind the boom by the current coming around the bend in the river.

At the down stream end of the boom, they were directed into a bull chain by the workers. The bull chain was a heavy, wooden V shaped frame resembling a flume, with a large electric powered chain in the bottom, with dogs sticking up to catch the logs. It would bring them up the bank, under the highway, and out on a platform on the millpond side of the damn. The platform was probably fifteen feet above the pond level and had a slanting ramp on the north side. The logs would be kicked off the chain and would roll down the ramp into the water with an impressive splash. We, the dam kids, walked this way to school and I'm sure there was more than one tardiness caused by the spectacle.

The whole area was off limits, but there was no fence and no one around much of the time, so we walked the boom and ran the logs up the river, and climbed on and swam off the pond end of the chain. I collected many slivers in my bare feet from the slivery wood it was made of. A group of pilings in the south east corner of the millpond is all that is left of this structure.

The pond was much larger then than it is now. Someone has filled in a significant segment at the north and west ends for one of the subsequent mill operations, including where the present metal building is sited. For the most part it was off limits except during the winter when it was frozen over, but again there were many times when there was no one around to enforce this ban. When winter threatened, the lumber company would raise and lower the water level to break up the ice so they could use the pond as long as possible. But eventually they would give up and the pond would belong to the town.

For many years the ice was cut as soon as it would freeze to about a foot thick, and hauled up town and stored in ice houses. These were wooden buildings with double walls about a foot thick, with sawdust in between for insulation. Sawdust was a waste product then, mostly burned in the mill's burners, so additional sawdust was heaped over the ice for the same reason. Ice stored this way would last through most of the summer.

The saws used were similar to those used for logging, except shorter and slightly thicker so they were stiff, and with handles only on one end, and were filed with no set to the teeth. After cutting, the blocks of ice would be grasped with large tongs and pulled up the hill by horses early on, and later by trucks. Bunn Hambrook who had the transfer and storage company in town had an ice house out behind his store at one point.

At night, half the town would be on the ice on skates. Fires would be built on shore and also well out on the ice as they were the only light available. Sometimes when the ice was thick enough, a car would be chained at both ends and driven out on the ice, and a long line of people would form behind it and play crack the whip.

When the company would raise and lower the water level at the beginning of the winter, it would leave cracks in the ice after it got too thick to break totally. I was on the end of one of these whips one night and was traveling faster than I could control. My skate dropped into one of these cracks and stopped. It jerked my skate off my shoe and I ended up skating on my face. Don't ever let anyone tell you ice can't get hot. I got back to the fire and found the front of my face all bloody. I didn't discover I had broken off half of a front tooth until I got home and faced my mother, who no longer became excited over a little of my blood, but did over the broken tooth.

Finances being what they were, nothing was done about the tooth and I lived with half a tooth for a couple years until it eventually became ulcerated. We made a trip to Metaline one night in the dark to see the only dentist in the area. This was my first and only while in Ione, trip to a dentist and didn't make me want to go back for seconds.

He said it was ulcerated and he couldn't pull the tooth or use any pain killer until it was drained as the tooth was in the upper front and the poison could go directly up into my brain. So he pulled out a scalpel and lanced it so it would drain, and had me come back about a week later when he pulled the tooth. I think the total cost was five dollars. The tooth never was replaced until the Air Corps did so several years later.

Most skates then were not like today. Unless you were more affluent than most, both ice and roller skates were adjustable for size and had clamps that tightened them by the use of a key, onto the sole of your shoe. Sometimes they would, under enough stress, pull the entire sole off the shoe, much to the distaste of the parent who got to replace the shoes for the affluent, and the shoe soles only at the home of the less so.

At our house, this would usually mean the shoes would be repaired by Ole as there usually wasn't money for new shoes or to pay the shoemaker to make the needed repairs. Most of our shoes were resoled several times until we outgrew them or the leather of the sides wore out.

CHAPTER IX

About the time we moved to the house off Sullivan Lake Road, we acquired a little sister. The youngest child, with three older brothers, she was destined to achieve most spoiled status fairly quickly. We, the spoilers, noticed little difference. For us life depended more on the seasons than on such matters.

One of the few things I see today as being larger than I remember it, is the pond in the lower part of our yard. We built crude rafts for collecting things like turtles, frogs, or tadpoles. The water wasn't deep, because more than once the raft would fall apart and we would end up walking out through the mud. In winter it would freeze over and we would skate, sans skates, on the ice. Everyone, except kids, is aware that ice that has reeds and grass growing up through it is not very sound. We never believed this when told, so we also ended up walking home with cold wet feet more than once in the winter. No one ever owned more than one pair of shoes, so wet shoes lined up by the stove or even in the oven while they dried in preparation for school the next day was a common sight.

Contrarily, another thing from memory definitely seems smaller. The bank along the north side of Sullivan must have been much higher as we used to play there with toy cars and dig tunnels into the ground for garages. Also on the north side of the road was the Henshaw family house, where there is now a large pile of gravel. I used to sympathize with these kids. They were constantly taunted with various butcherings of their name, Henhouse being one of the nicer.

There were traces of a road that went down through the woods from the southeast corner of the yard. At the other end of it was the Ione Gun Club, on the bluff overlooking the river. This was another of those forbidden places we chose to play as it was seldom used by club members during the week. We spent hours digging the lead out of the rifle and pistol firing butts. This we would melt down in tin cans, heated in open fires, to form larger chunks of lead, for reasons that now elude me, if there ever were any. I don't remember ever doing anything productive with it.

There was an old log house at the south end they used for a club house or some unknown to us purpose, with firing stands built on the porch. We could usually find an occasional live cartridge in the area of the stands from which they fired the rifles, or closer to the butts from where they fired the pistols, so we always had a collection of various calibers of live bullets to play with.

In the area between the house and the rifle butts was the shotgun shooting range. There were several small wooden shelters that were half buried in the ground, so a man could crouch inside and launch the clay pigeons, and a man behind the shed could shoot at them over the launchers head with a shotgun. We had about as much use for the missed clay pigeons as for the lead, but we collected any unbroken ones we could find anyway. We also collected the occasional unfired shotgun shell that had been dropped. They were more fun.

We discovered that many of the shotgun shells would fit inside of a three quarter inch water pipe.

Then after much experimentation, we figured out that if one would drill a small hole in the center of a pipe cap, screw it on over the shotgun shell, insert a nail in the hole and hit the nail with a two by four, the shell would fire.

Drilling was a time consuming operation as we only had a hand drill and probably a dull bit, but we had lots of time. The drill was sort of like an old fashioned egg beater, with a hand crank on the side. By trial and error we also figured out that the pipe must be fastened securely to a fence post or it would travel backward about as fast as the shot went forward. It never occurred to us that the pipe might not hold the pressure, and blow up in our faces. Mom never caught on, but on occasion she would come outside at the sound to puzzle over who was shooting a gun so close to the house.

From the south end of the gun club there was a crude road, no longer existing as near as I can determine, that ran along the north fence of the cemetery and out to the highway. Don't imagine we ever got brave enough to use it after dark.

Our cows also found the gun club irresistible. As I mentioned before, they just considered a fence a challenge and the grass along the river a delicacy. We spent many hours along the river, but were never interested in going there for a productive reason like fetching the cows. And the cows were just as reluctant to do anything that we might want, like going home at milking time without a lot of urging. I recall one instance when I found one of our cows walking down the highway, across the dam toward town. I tried to turn her toward home and she just jumped the guard rail and continued in her original direction. I jumped the rail and grabbed her tail with one hand and the rail with the other and tried to hold her. She headed down the side of the dam, pulled loose, and just kept going. Rails at the time were steel cable run through wooden posts alongside the road.

These cows supplied us with milk, butter, and a calf for meat on the years they produced a bull calf, but I'm not sure it would have been possible to convince us kids they were worth the effort required to live with them. Besides chasing them all over the country, they had to be milked twice daily and their barn cleaned more often than we wanted to do so.

We sold milk, that I usually got to deliver, for if memory serves, fifty cents a gallon. It was delivered in large mouth gallon glass jars that originally held pickles I think, on an exchange basis. Take a full one and pick up yesterday's empty. We sold butter churned from cream skimmed off the milk we didn't sell, for twenty five cents a pound.

We churned the butter by sitting and bouncing the cream on our knee, in a quart jar. It would take about half an hour to churn a jar full and we would reap about half a pound of butter from a quart of cream. The folks would drink the buttermilk left over, but I never developed a taste for it. One butter customer that I remember delivering to was the Wrights who lived across the highway at the top of the hill to the south, now the home of an auto repair shop.

As I previously mentioned, we had acquired a 1927 Chevrolet Sedan sometime after moving to the big house. Once in a while we would load everyone in the car and visit Ole's mother in Kettle falls. Three boys in the rear seat and two adults and little sister in front. No one told us to feel deprived because we had no seat belts, but then people were deemed to have the right to run their own life.

It was a long trip. Low gear all the way up the Tiger hill. The hill is just as high now, but the road has been much improved, as have the cars. I have heard stories of earlier cars, Ford Ts, that had to turn around and back up the hill as they had a vacuum gas feed that wasn't strong enough to pump gas up hill from the rear mounted tank, while climbing the hill at the slow speeds. The road to Colville was oiled gravel and not much more than one lane, and winding.

I remember one story of some young guys who were coming down Tiger Hill in an old Dodge. They went off the road in the snow and ended up, upside down, between roads at one of the sharp corners. They merely got out and rolled the car over another time or two and ended up on the road below and proceeded on home. I believe this was attributed to the Weaver boys but its one of those stories you hear but never really confirm.

Sometimes we stopped at Ole's sister Goldie's house in Colville. She was married to Clarence Reed, a brother of Loren of Ione. Again, memory is dim, but I believe Clarence was later killed in a logging truck accident.

Grandma Ole, as we referred to her, lived in a nice to us, two story house along the highway in Kettle Falls. This was before Grand Coulee dam was constructed. Her house was later moved up the hill to the present site of Kettle Falls, when the dam flooded out the original town site in the late thirties. We boys were never very comfortable in her house. She had numerous fancy knick-knacks sitting around on every flat surface, displayed on clean white crocheted doilies and looking very fragile, so we were afraid to move around them, or touch anything.

And she had indoor plumbing. We had encountered indoor plumbing at school where a long enamel trough, long enough for a dozen or so boys to line up, along one wall, had water running through it all of the time. But had never seen it in a house. If you flushed the toilet it made a lot of noise so everybody knew what you were doing, and if you didn't flush it was worse. Fortunately, there was a large billboard across the highway and not a lot of traffic passing by on the highway so we managed.

CHAPTER X

It was a long walk to school from the house on Sullivan for grade school kids, in the neighborhood of a mile, and apparently school busses hadn't been discovered yet. At least by Ione. The school had other deficiencies as well. Locals apologized with the remark that we could not attract any good teachers and we couldn't afford to pay enough money to get any better.

The first couple years I wasn't aware. Guess I was too small to come to the notice of the town kids at first. But this didn't last for long. By the time I was in the fourth grade they were laying for us and making us run the gauntlet to get across the dam on the way home.

As previously mentioned. the lumber yard stretched from the mill up to the edge of town and was useful for eluding them. The east edge of the yard, about on a line with the highway through town, was where the workers stacked the lath. There were two double stacks. Each stack was composed of two stacks of bundled lath, about two feet apart, with a roof over both of them, forming a tunnel approximately a block long, with only occasional openings out from the center. I got rather good at negotiating them in a hurry and dodging the lath that stuck out of the piles everywhere, waiting in the semi-dark for the unwary.

The problem came when you reached the south end of the pile. There was nothing left but the bald bank of the pond. Many times when pressed I elected to run the logs in the pond. This means traveling across the individual logs floating free in the water and only works well when they are confined so they are fairly tight together.

One time my pursuers stuck to the booms, the long way around, so I was gaining until I ran out of logs. I had been paying more attention to my rear than the logs in front which was a big mistake. Suddenly I was on the last log and it was too small to support me if I stopped, and there was several feet of open water ahead. My log sank, so I flopped through the water to the boom. It wasn't late enough in the year for the water to be frozen, but almost. I would have sworn it was freezing on me as I clambered up the steep bank at the south side of the pond, up through the brush, and walked the rest of the way home wet to the armpits. I remember the looks of puzzlement on the faces of some of the people, when I dripped my way through their yards.

Teachers were no help. To them we were the damn kids also. I still remember when one stood at the front of the class and called me down because I, "Came to school in jeans that were so patched that I looked like someone had shot me in the rear with a shotgun."

The trees in the parking strip in front of the school were planted by the students for arbor day one year. The ones that now look like malformed dwarfs where they have been chopped down to keep them out of the power lines. I don't remember my age at the time, but I had charge of the water hose. One of the girls asked me to wash off the blade of the shovel she was using. I looked up and saw the man, one of only two male teachers we had, who was coach, teacher, and principal, bearing down on me.

Apparently he was misunderstanding my actions

and thought the girl was defending herself from the water with the shovel. I could see he had blood in his eye and wouldn't be interested in listening to any explanation. I dropped the hose and took off running toward the baseball field on the west side of the school, with him kicking me in the rear end every time he caught up with me, all the way around the bases.

Actually it wasn't all one way and totally undeserved. In winter we were forbidden to throw snow balls out in front of the school. A dozen or so of us were in the area, actually the road off the school grounds to the west, at noon time, with a good battle going when we spotted the principal walking back from town. He stopped to give us a good chewing, I though aimed particularly at me although I was one of the youngest, and turned to continue on to the school.

I made as if to throw a snowball at his retreating figure and someone said they dared me. I was never very accurate with a ball, but could never refuse a dare. But on this day I was deadly. I knocked his hat right off his head. He whirled around to see who dared, and everyone was standing looking at me in awe, so he knew. I think he must have been unsettled by the act and the daring involved, as I don't recall any punishment resulting directly from it, except the anticipation I lived with.

My grandparents still lived on Huckleberry Mountain and we spent quite a bit of time there. Especially in the summer. We still wandered. We played in the Model T Ford in an old pole barn behind the house in which at Jimmy Kinette had died. I've always heard all Fords were plain black, but this one was much fancier and well decorated with brass. I always wondered where it ended up when the government bought out the property on the hill. Car collecting was another thing that came later.

There were two other old homesteads about a half mile further down the same road that were still standing, partially. They had apple trees near the house, and fields that I assume had grown nothing more than wild hay. We usually had at least one twenty-two rifle with us in our travels and there were lots of gophers in the fields to practice on. I was never sure how accurate our aim was, as the squirrels always disappeared down the holes whether hit or not.

We also found an old powder shed at one of the places that had a half case of old dynamite in it. We spent all of an afternoon trying to get the dynamite to do something. We set it up and shot at it several times and nothing happened so we built a fire and threw it in. It wouldn't even burn. We finally gave up in disgust and left it lay.

I heard later, that old dynamite was very unstable and had to be handled carefully because the good part is nitroglycerin and it settles to the bottom where it concentrates to almost pure nitroglycerin. Maybe there is a cutoff point where it becomes too old to do anything and we were lucky. And maybe it all just drained into the ground under the shed and we could have blown up the whole shed by shooting into the ground. Who knows?

Another memory is of standing in the doorway of the barn at my grandparent's place, behind the cows, and watching one of my uncles milk the cow. I didn't find it funny then, but time mellows everything. One of the cows had diarrhea and coughed. She painted my outline on the wall of the barn, and everyone but me and my mother who had to bathe, me thought it hilarious. I suspect she also got a laugh from it when

I was no longer around.

On one such trip, returning down from the hill we stopped at an old house about half way down. This was the same house that my mother found the bottles for her ill fated root beer experiment in our first house on the hill. There were some parts for manikins, from I know not what defunct enterprise.

I selected a woman's head, carried it home, and took it upstairs, where I placed it atop the post at the top of the steps. I considered it quite funny that my younger brothers were afraid to go up stairs with it there. That is I thought it funny until it got dark up there, and the folks told me to go up and remove it so the kids could go to bed. Turning on the light involved going all the way up past it and pulling a string, and I was also afraid to go up there in the dark. After much recrimination, I think it was my step dad who finally went up and got it so we would go to bed. Not sure what ever happened to the head.

CHAPTER XI

My oldest brother Ray joined me at school in 1935 and my youngest brother Arnold followed in 1937. For better or worse they got to follow in my footsteps and carry on in spite of any reputation I may have garnered at the school, but at least they had an older brother so they escaped some of the pressure.

Somewhere in this time span WPA happened and many things in the town changed.

The school got a new gymnasium that I only assume was one result. This was a basketball floor, small by today's standards but quite grand for the times, with a stage at one side. The basement had a kitchen, hot lunches were five cents. A large multi-purpose room ran down the east side, and the wood shop was in the northwest corner. All of the basement rooms had raw cement walls. At one of the dances held there, I don't remember who, but one of the guys got mad and took a swing at me. I ducked and he slid his knuckles across the wall and left a lot of his skin on the rough cement. I still can picture him standing there gripping his bleeding hand and sucking on his knuckles. Took all thoughts of fighting out of him.

The Gym was used for the usual basketball and PE classes in winter, as well as becoming the center for a number of social activities for the whole town. I remember being in the chorus of Pirates of Penzance on the stage, and attending a Halloween dance in the big room downstairs with me dressed as a girl. Spent the whole night dodging boys and their raging hormones. Fancy dances were held upstairs on the basketball floor.

With a total of only about seventy five students in high school, Ione had enough boys to field a basketball team that went to state occasionally, but could only manage enough players for six man football. Eleven men on a team and another team to practice against would have used every boy in the school. The two basketball games I remember best were the time the locals were embarrassed by the antics of the Globe Trotters, and another game where they played against a team who played while riding on donkeys.

Another event that brought out most of the town was the magician. He demonstrated liquid oxygen by dipping cranberries into the tank and then throwing them out over the crowd to show how quick the berries had frozen to the point they shattered. The problem came when they thawed, and of course were walked on, on the shiny new hardwood floors.

Of course there was the obligatory Christmas program and a large decorated tree in the back of the gym each year. I remember passing through the line and receiving a red net sack, like an onion sack, with an orange and some hard candy in it. Nobody thought of the candy needing to be wrapped. Also nobody thought to object on the grounds that the religious theme at school was unconstitutional and might corrupt us so there were no law suits.

Things began looking up financially for the family also. Ole continued to work wherever he could find employment. Mostly as a truck driver, but occasionally in logging. One such was a logging camp that he stayed at and only came home on week-ends. I remember his only complaint was about some of the fare served in the chow hall.

Most of the guys were Scandinavian and their

tastes were different from his. The worst in his opinion was the head cheese. A pickled pigs head was set on a platter in the center of the table, snout up, and the men cut off slices with their pocket knives to munch on. He said, "I don't care where you sit around the table, that damn thing is sitting there staring at you."

The town's swimming pool was built by the WPA and Ole got on there for a while. Not sure why we needed a pool as we swam in both the mill pond and the river. We swam in the pool also after it was built, mostly for social reasons. Mostly because that's where all of the girls went I believe, but we complained about the chlorine.

My mother worked in the Dean Grocery building, showing others how to make mattresses, after the store closed early in the thirties. The mattresses were made for free, by the eventual owners, with farm surplus materials furnished by the government. I don't remember hearing whether she were paid for working there or not, but we did work there also and we did sleep on one of the mattresses for several years.

My mother also worked as a practical nurse, sometimes at the hospital on Houghton, operated by Dr. Canning, and sometimes as a live in nurse for home care of mostly pneumonia patients. I'm not sure if she worked for the doctor for money or just to keep up with the doctor bills I incurred. I did manage to incur them regularly, winter or summer.

There was a ski jump located on the hillside on Cedar Creek Road, just beyond the bridge, across from the little old house that is still there. The hill was high, and very steep. At the top they built a wooden tower, much of it merely saplings nailed together, for a run to the jump. There were no ski lifts. The jumpers would climb the hill, then climb the ladder to the top of the tower, with their skis on their shoulders. They would then come down the narrow run with a rush to the jump. The good ones would jump almost to the bottom of the hill and have a very short distance in which to stop. I remember being surprised at the time by the fact that skiers traveled great distances to participate, although I'm not sure where they came from. But great distances was relative. To me, Colville was another world and I'm not sure if where they came from was any farther away. Northport would have sounded foreign to me.

Some of us boys would go up when the hill wasn't being used for skiing and run down the hill on sleds. Sort of play chicken as it were. Each would try to go higher on the hill than the last. I was never willing to be beaten, so to show everyone up, I went all the way up to the bottom of the jump, meaning I couldn't be bested. The hill was prepared by the skiers climbing the hill sidewise on their skis, so it was a series of ridges that had frozen to ice. A rather rough and very steep surface for sledding.

I was doing somewhere around ninety I'm sure when the sled got away from me and turned sidewise. The down hill runner caught in a rut and folded under, and I went the rest of the way down the hill on my face. I relearned the fact that ice can get hot. I rubbed the skin off my face, just deep enough for the white portion of the blood to seep, very little actual red blood. Doc Canning thought it funny when he got to tend it.

In the fall, fruit peddlers used to come through town with fruit from Yakima on their old trucks. Ione had a sign saying, Green River Ordinances Enforced, at the city limits. Not sure by whom, as we only had a marshal some of the time. This meant that going door to door was illegal. They found a way around it by hiring couple of local boys to go door to door and have interested people come out to the truck. Not sure how this differed, but supposedly it was legal or at least okay.

After doing the town in the hot weather, not sure how successfully as he still had a lot of fruit, he said he was going to Aladdin and would bring us back afterwards if we would ride along to do the same thing there. Again, roads must have been changed since then as he headed out Cedar Creek Road for Aladdin and that road doesn't go anyplace now.

Just beyond the ski jump where the road goes up the hill, we saw several boys heading up the creek far below, us with fishing poles. Being good buddies we pitched a few apples over the side to them. We obviously forgot about rear view mirrors. When the man yelled and stopped the truck we bailed out and jumped down the hill to where the other guys were. I didn't notice, but there was a barb wire fence stretched across the hillside. It was about half way down so I had time to build up my speed, and it was hidden in the bushes. Somehow I stepped though it and then fell over the top so I was caught hanging head down with my leg trapped between the twisted wires.

This again resulted in me making several trips to see Doc Canning. It stripped most of the skin off my left shin and then it became infected. He had to cut it open again and remove something that always made me think of chicken guts. We didn't remember until later, but we never did get paid for our work.

Actually, come to think, my mother wasn't the

only one to work to pay for my deeds. Ole worked for a while, pumping gas at Browns Shell Station, on the corner of Main and the highway, to pay for the big plate glass window I broke when I pegged a large chunk of ice at a kid's head and he ducked. Never really forgave the guy that duck, but Ole said he was glad I hit the window rather than his head as it was probably a lot cheaper to repair.

CHAPTER XII

In the thirties, money was a scarce commodity for kids also. We used to patrol the highway both ways from town as well as the town dump picking up bottles for the deposits. A penny each bottle except for some of the larger sizes that were a bonanza at five cents. Cans that are much easier to handle and much lighter hadn't been invented yet.

We thought it directed at our enterprise when some form of plastic bottle was designed. They had, "No deposit, No return," molded into their sides. But they looked close to the same as the glass ones so we tried to slip them in the mix anyway and felt we had made a great victory when we got away with it.

In season we could generally find an occasional lawn to mow. The usual pay was about twenty five cents, fifty cents for a real big one, and the mowers were the old reel push type. Stacking a cord of wood into the woodshed brought about the same. Of course candy bars that were bigger by far than today's two or three for a dollar size were a nickel. One I remember, purchased often, not for its taste but for its size, was the Big Hunk. It was white nougat, with peanuts, and almost half inch thick, about three inches wide, and nearly eight inches long. Several others like Mr. Goodbar and Babe Ruth were almost as large.

Greenhouse Road, I assume it got its name from the farm and greenhouse located on it, was another source for the lucky. I don't remember the road having the name, but I did work at Cook's farm and greenhouse located there, for a short time. Most of the local kids worked there picking strawberries or other crops at one time or other. They had a hard and fast rule that one had to be at least thirteen years old to work. I was big for my age and at age eleven was doing okay until one of the girls got in trouble for throwing berries. When they fired her she ratted me out. This was to be my bicycle money. I had worked for about a two weeks and the pay due me was six dollars. I knew it wouldn't buy much of a bike, even then.

I rode to Spokane with Ole on a lumber trip and we went to a used bike shop. They only had one bike they would sell for six dollars. It had no fenders, and was of the old out of favor balloon tire variety. I know Ole felt bad because he couldn't help me, but I didn't expect it. We loaded the bike on the back of the truck and he stopped at the top of the last hill before home, in front of the Wright's, and I rode the bike the rest of the way home. Wish I could say I was proud of it, but I did ride it for several years.

I am again vague on the exact dates, but this was about the time of the strike that effectively eliminated Ione as we knew it. As we walked the highway to and from school, we passed the men who were camped out where the entry road from the mill joined the highway, beside the millpond. They were there for a long time, but I mostly remember them being out there, with a fire in a fifty five gallon barrel for heat, throughout the whole winter. The lumber in the yard was slowly sold off, and the piles gradually shrunk as they sat and froze.

Trucks and heavy cranes showed up one day and Alaska Junk from Seattle and Portland proceeded to dismantle the mill. The jobs of most of Ione went down the highway with the departing trucks. The railroad used to run across a trestle and through the mill, and I believe they also took part of the rails out as the railroad seemed to disappear also, but maybe this was only from lack of freight to haul. It was widely rumored that the scrap went to Japan for later return in other forms, but this may have only been part of the strike rhetoric.

The large red buildings of the mill sat there for several years before they were gradually removed for their lumber. Then all that was left was a very tall smoke stack from the scrap burner. I believe it stayed there until well after WW2.

When the mill went, so did Ione's electric supply. The town acquired a large Diesel generator that ran day and night, and sat at the south end of Central street where the fire station is today. It was several years later, years after Grand Coulee Dam was built, that outside power reached Ione via the Rural Electrification Agency.

The changes on the human level were even of more import to us kids at the time, as we watched our lifelong friends disappear one family at a time. Usually they would just not be at school, no explanation. When families like the Oscarsons with their twelve kids, a couple of whom were about my age and special friends, left it was definitely noticeable.

The dams in The Pend Oreille River hadn't been built, so the water level fluctuated greatly. The area where the Ione Motel resides was a gravel pit and the river swirled through it at high water times. There was several yards of bank exposed along the area during low water times. In the area where the sewage treatment plant is located the water formed several areas that became like lakes as the high water receded. Here it was trapped and was warmed to swimming temperature while the river was still icy.

This one I remember well. The Congregational Church held vacation bible school in early June, as they probably still do. Several of us, I think four, played hookey from Sunday School and rode our bikes out to this area to swim. The water was great after one reached the warm pools, but it was necessary to wade through some waist high, very cold flows that were very swift to get there.

I was still only at the dog paddle stage and when I started back I missed the sandbar and was swept out into the river. We yelled back and forth and someone started to go for help, but no one present swam much better than I and other help was at least half an hour away. I knew I was lost and relaxed and let the current take me.

Next thing I knew my feet hit bottom, but I was on the other side of the river. I was on the east bank, almost frozen, about three miles down river from the bridge, almost to box canyon, and we had been skinny dipping. Luckily the few houses along that side of the river were abandoned and our house was the first one on the west side of the bridge. Somehow I even managed to get into the house without being discovered by mom. My bike and clothes were still down there so I later had to walk all of the way back down to retrieve them.

The bridge at that time was all wood. The wooden truss work underneath was designed for climbing. At least we climbed it. I earlier mentioned the boom that ran up the river to catch logs. It ran under and connected to the bridge piling. When the river was high it was possible to climb down the trusses and get on it, or with difficulty climb back up. At low water there was too much bare creosote pole exposed below the cross members so it was beyond us. Since we were barefoot most any time there wasn't snow on the ground, we picked up our share of slivers off the timbers and booms that the workers walked with cork boots. The creosote slivers were particularly painful.

One other river related experience comes to mind. The pond emptied into the river through a flume under the road as it does now, but then it was wooden and built up on a trestle that was very un-level and extended about fifty feet beyond the road. It was winter and the flow was minimal, sort of wandered down the flume, leaving islands on alternate sides that held snow and ice. One also held a rabbit that I decided to rescue.

I walked down inside the flume and he appeared to acquiesce so I picked him up by the ears, put him under my coat, and climbed over the side and down to the river bank. I then reached under the coat to lift him out and he nailed me on my middle finger. He hung on until I lifted him out by his teeth. He then let go and took off without a word of thanks, leaving me with a bloody finger that some of my friends happily suggested would probably lead to some terrible disease. I'd be lucky if it didn't do anything worse than just fall off.

TOUR OF IONE

Now I would like to take time out and lead you on a tour of Ione, as I knew it some seventy years ago. Mostly because I have been asked to prepare a map and I can't figure out how to make it fit in the small space I have available and still have it be readable. Some others saw it differently than I, and have brought their views to my attention, but these views are mine, shared or not.

Most places around the world have doubled and doubled again in population. Ione's population has changed as economics changed, but its numbers have changed little. I look around and see only a scant half dozen of my schoolmates still living in the area, most others leaving as mills closed, being replaced by others as the mines opened, and later changing again when the mines closed and smaller mills were built, to keep the population fairly constant.

Beginning at the foot of Main Street at the river. The ferry that was here actually predated my time in Ione, having been replaced by the bridge built about a mile south in about 1930. Many changes were wrought in the city park shortly after. The pool and many other improvements were thanks to the WPA of the Roosevelt era. The pool then had no cover, but stayed relatively busy in summer, even with the many other places in the area to swim. I think this was mostly because that's where the girls hung out so that's where the boys hung also. In those days, boys chased girls, until the girls caught them, somewhat different than today.

The hill leading down to the park was busy in

winter, being close to town and both long enough an steep enough for interesting sledding, and probably too steep and slick for cars. The residents of the house on the north at the hill top helped by hosing down the hill at night so it would freeze up and be extremely fast and popular for sledding. My memories are of starting under the street light at the top and ripping down the hill, half afraid of what I was doing, into the darkness of the park. And then the long, cold, trip pulling the sled back up the hill into the light.

The block between First Avenue and Highway 31 hasn't changed much. A couple of houses have disappeared and a couple others have been replaced by manufactureds. On the corner at the highway, The Ione Theater, now The Baptist Church, was on the North side. On the South side was Shackleton's Texaco station and garage and Greyhound Bus Depot and General Motors Agency. I think it was the 1936 Chevrolet five passenger coupe that caught our eye. But who could ever afford it at $537.

This was a huge wood frame building extending back to the alley on the south, with wood and dirt floors, and with living quarters for the family on top. There were several kids, but my memory only brings up three names. Bruce, Wayne, and Patty. Wayne I remember because of the 22 Hi Standard pistol he owned. He used to shoot it at the feet of the other kids and make them dance, a penitentiary offense now, but receiving little note then. Patty I remember for other reasons.

The next block up, between the highway and Central, had Browns Shell on the North corner in what would be the parking lot of the present closed grocery. In what would be an invitation to a law suit today, it had an open pit lube rack beside the sidewalk on the highway side. Up the hill from it was the Ione Garage, a rather large and rickety wooden building. There was a restaurant next to it, but it disappeared fairly early on so I don't remember for sure, but I think it was Goade's. The corner where the I.O.O.F. hall now stands was vacant.

On the south corner at the highway was Deans Grocery Store. Most of the older residents remember Deans for the penny candy case that they spent lots of time pressing their nose on. My clearest memory is that it was the only place in town where Margerine could be purchased, although it was illegal for a Washington store to stock it. It was also an early casualty of the mill closing.

Later, as part of one of the relief programs, I think NRA, there was a self serve mattress factory here. People could go there and make their own mattresses from materials provided by the government. Mostly with cotton from farm surpluses and heavy, canvas like, striped cloth that was probably surplus from somewhere else. For most people, these mattresses would be replacing straw filled burlap ticks, as they were at our house. I don't know if she were paid or not, but my mother was one of the teachers who helped the mattress makers.

Ione was platted into twenty five foot lots on all of the commercial streets and most of the buildings in town were narrow and deep, and most had uneven fir floors. Many of them had living quarters above the stores. I don't remember ever being in most, probably because I seldom had money to spend.

Next to Deans was a vacant lot where I suffered the first sneak attack by the Japanese. Mary Terroka, at about age eight, slipped up behind me and larruped me over the head with a length of two by four for arguing with her sister Grace.

Next was Hambrook's Transfer and Storage. Owned by Bunn Hambrook, father of Donna Hambrook Bell who is still with us and was kind enough to furnish many of the photos that will be used in the book as well as helping with my short memory. At one time he had an ice house somewhere out behind this business. They lived in a log house on the highway, where the parking for the Food Court Store is now. To my knowledge, I was never in his building, but when we left Ione we used his services to ship the few things we took with us. We rode the bus and he delivered our heavy luggage to the train depot in Spokane. One of the last memories is of my mother handing the 40-65 rifle that I coveted, over to him, and asking him to get it to Doc Canning who had moved to Colville.

Next was Steckers Mercantile, by descendents of one of Ione's first settlers, and sellers of many of the work clothes of the loggers and mill workers of the area.

The Ione Steam Laundry was next. It was a long narrow room that was always hot and sweaty. The laundry started in large machines at the rear and worked its way toward the front by different routes depending on what it consisted of. Sheets were fed into a system of wide belts on rollers and came out the other end partially folded. Clothing items took a different route to the hand pressing machines on the other side of the room. I can picture Harold Matsuda standing at one of the large ironers that spouted steam up around him when he closed the top and stepped on the lever beneath. Perhaps this explains why the place was always hot and sweaty. The steam came from large wood fired boilers, that burned four foot long cord wood, in the rear of the building. The five members of the Terroka family, and Frank lived upstairs. Probably very comfortable in winter, but I'm sure not so in summer. Hambrooks and the laundry were used by the local fire department for practice burns, I believe in the 1960s.

Betty's Ione State bank was on the corner of Central. I guess that wasn't the official name but it was known locally as Betty's Bank. It's still there and still in business, but the name has changed more than once. One of mighty few businesses in Ione then who have survived until now. Fred Trumbull, Attorney, who was also city attorney, had an office in the same building, behind the bank.

On Central Avenue to the north, on the east side of the street, the building where the Town Hall is now located, until recently the library, was the Water and Light building. Managed by Elmer Widger, who also ran the theater, as mentioned elsewhere in this epic. Across Houghton was the school on which I have dwelt at length.

On the west side of the street, on the alley, across from the Dukeshires, the house where I now live, where it would be about number 103 N. Central today, was a small Ladies Wear Shop. The building, probably originally a small house, is totally gone. On the corner of Houghton, labeled Ione Town Hall was the telephone building. Phone numbers at the time were like 18N or 16W and as far as I have been able to ascertain there was no separation between Ione and Newport in the numbers. In fact 18N was Ione and I believe 18V was Newport. The little building out behind, labeled dog pound now, was a telephone switching station.

Across Houghton Street, on the northwest corner was the Ione Town Hall, in a building about the size and shape of a single car garage, possibly originally another small house. Beside it and about half as big was the fire department, I think its building is still in existence, but unmarked. Fire equipment consisted of a single, hand hose cart pulled by a men via a tongue in front. It had a hand pump operated by rails on each side, and carried rolls of hose and other fire tools between. Beside the town hall to the north was the fire tower, a building about ten feet square and two stories tall. I understand, the old fire bell now resides at ground level down in the city park.

To the south of Main St. on Central Avenue, the only places worth note were the house on the south east corner of Blackwell where we lived, in an old store front, the center house across from us where Zelva Boyer lived, and the diesel power plant that operated night and day, located where the fire department is today.

The area above Central Avenue is more difficult. The number of businesses was higher and there was more flux. Businesses have come and gone and buildings as well. On the north side of the street, the building now housing the variety store was originally only half there. There was a vacant space on the corner. There was a variety store, Stevens Jewelry Store, the Post Office moved from the NW corner of fourth in Beardsley's Grocery, to the space now the Video Store, sometime about 1934, and George Moe's Ice Cream Parlor was in the space occupied by today's restaurant bar.

Moe's was the hangout of most of the kids. It is where I learned about fountain Cherry Cokes and Green Rivers, then priced at five cents, and banana splits at a quarter when I could scrounge up the money. It was the place we could cheer on some of the older boys on the pinball machines, one of which cost Harold Matsuda when he tried to use tokens instead of coins. The magic age for being able to play the pin-balls must have been eighteen.

Somewhere in the mix there was another jeweler named W. B. Sweet, Dr. Scott Matheson, Dentist, at one point George Lundeen's Grocery was on the corner where the phone company is now if memory is right, until they moved to larger quarters. Ione had five groceries I believe, but not all necessarily at the same time. One business I would think us kids would remember, but I don't, was Sherman and Davis, Funeral home. It was here, but I have no memory of it. Some of these are vague memories so some of these stores could have spilled West across fourth Avenue.

On the south side of Main Street, on the corner was The Pend Oreille Hotel on which I have already expended considerable ink. After a blank space, Hansen's Bakery came next, I also described my work there. I have been told it burned down in the sixties, and wouldn't be too surprised because of the setup of the oven. Then there was a small clothing store, The Toggery, that may be the small addition on the east side of the present hardware store.

I think the hardware store has been constant, but has changed hands several times so the name depends on the date. Early it was R.B. Hall's Hardware. At some point it became Vickerman's Hardware. Now The Country Hardware, and probably something else in between. Then came Albert's Billiard Hall, once the Country Billiards, I believe it was the source of the tokens we found when the wooden sidewalks were replaced, and hasn't strayed to far as it is now a tavern

I guess one might refer to it as the great barbershop mystery. There was a man named Foy who was "a" or "the" Ione barber, depending on who you ask. His contemporaries refer to him as a good barber, but decline to comment on him further, on the premise that if you can't say nice don't say. I have seen written word from his family stating he was Ione's only barber. They also say his shop was in the small building above fourth, with the historic label of a cedar company affixed. I have no particular memories of barbers as we had our own. My mother and her hand clippers, hair pulling clippers that is, took care of all such needs at our house. But, there was a barber shop sandwiched in between the billiard hall and the next store, that I think was Blazer's, a second hardware store then, which would indicate the family are mistaken, either in his location or in the number of barbers in town.

In the now empty space next to the west was a store, Robert Hale's clothing store I think, and then Mat Cleary's restaurant that was the hangout of the slightly older than high school crowd. I delivered bread and rolls to them from the bakery. On the corner was Jayne's Drugstore and soda fountain. I understand that George Moe moved across the street and operated this fountain at a later date, but I think this was after I left town.

West across fourth on the north side was Beardsley's Grocery and Feed Store, another of my bakery customers. It had a butcher shop along the west side with a long glass case displaying various cuts of meat, where it was possible to get a bone for a dog, with meat enough for a pot of soup still clinging to it, for free. I'm sure many of them never reached the dog until after they had been through the soup pot. The Post Office was in the corner of the store on the Fourth Street side before moving east. I think the grocery must have expanded into the space when the Post Office moved a block down the street. I have no recollection of any other businesses west of the grocery, but there probably was at least one. On fourth behind the grocery was another restaurant at one time, and behind it on the corner of Houghton was a very large house operated as a rooming house. It was the only "accommodations" in the town after the Hotel Pend Oreille closed.

On the south corner of Fourth and Main was Burgan's Grocery Store. It was also a complete grocery that had expanded into the building next to it at some point by cutting a hole in the walls between, as seemed to be the norm at the time. I believe they closed up about 1940 and became Burgan's Furniture Store in Spokane.

Another mystery. I met a man recently, who claimed his folks built an appliance store in this space after WW2 and were there until the building, and their business, burned down in late 1940's. I have also seem color photos of that building being burned by the fire department for practice in the 1960's, when it was the offices of Fred Trumbull, Attorney. As I've stated before, all memories do not agree. Also I have been told that Foy's Barber shop was on Fourth behind this store instead of on Main Street.

This block always had gaps. The tavern now there was around, and I believe there was another in the block. The small building labeled McCoy's Cedar Company, was the office for John C. McCoy's pole operation. His pole yard was located on the railroad south of town. The next building, now apartments, was I believe Peder Carlson's shoe repair shop. Where the Post Office and Grange building are now, the Peaceful Valley Grange had a large, two story building. The Grange was on the second floor and the lower floor had several uses. It was a large wooden floor that became a dance floor with the addition of music, a meeting hall, and I believe a roller rink on occasion. I recall attending a dance there, more to heckle the girls than to dance, and slipping out for a nip on a bottle of cheap wine that someone had hidden under the corner of the building.

Along Railroad Avenue, and the rail tracks, was the depot that has since migrated across the street to its present location. The railroad first arrived in Ione in 1909 when it was The Idaho & Washington Northern Railroad, at least partially owned by F.A. Blackwell, Attorney, of Spokane. Hence Blackwell Street. In the 1930s, my time in the area, it was the Milwaukee Railroad, and is now the Pend Oreille Valley. If there were any other names in between, I'm not aware of them. The depot was moved across the street to make room for the metal building now occupied by the Lions.

To the south of the station was a small tank farm owned by Shell Oil Co. To the north on Houghton street was Doc Canning's Hospital, where my mother worked at times as a practical nurse. It recently burned, which seems to be. the history of Ione. Many more buildings burn than are rebuilt.

Across the tracks where the new grade school is located was the Ione school track and ball field. I have been told that the Huckleberry Mountain School building was moved to town and is now the residence on the South West corner of Seventh and Houghton.

Rents paid by some of the businesses were; T.S.

Jayne, Jayne's Drug Store - $25.   W.S. Culver, Pool Hall - $26. Irl Higgs, Beer Hall - $25.   E. G. Garske, Dry Goods - $20. E. M. Beardsley, Grocery Store (Who also rented a space to the Post Office) - $30. But a large loaf of bread cost 15 cents at the time.

On the same theme; In the Post Office records are many books listing sales of Postal Money Orders and Postal Savings deposits. The amounts listed are humorous in today's economy. Very few money orders are for over five dollars, and many postal savings deposits are less than one dollar, with account balances generally below one hundred dollars.

I also have, somewhere in my junk, a pass book from a bank in Ballard, then a town north of Seattle but now part of the town. In 1927, shortly after I was born, my mother opened an account for me, in the amount of 25 cents. She also made another deposit about two months later for another 25 cents. No other deposits were ever added.

In my digging to find things to supplement my memory, I found a list of businesses prepared by the postmaster in 1934 to justify the move of the post office from inside Beardsley's Grocery Store into a building of it's own. These lists, typed by someone definitely not a typist, on a typewriter that needed a new ribbon, on the inside of some non-white envelopes that had been torn open, appears on the next page.

LIST OF BUSINESS HOUSES IN IONE,WN
AS OF MAY 3,1934.

PEDER CARLSON..   SHOE REPAIR
JOHN E MC CAOY   POLES AND POSTS
A FOY   BARBER
E.M.BEARDSLEY   GROCERIES-FEED
T.S.JAYNE   DRUGGIST
ROBERT HALE   DRY GOODS
MAT CLEARY   RESTAURANT
R.E.ARNOLD   MEAT MARKET
R.W.ARNOLD   BEER PARLOR
S.W.BLAZIER   GROCERIES-HDWE
AXEL OLSON   BARBER
W.S.CULVER   POOL HALL
VICKERMAN HDWE CO   HDWE
IONE BAKERY   BAKERY
PENDOREILLE HOTEL   HOTEL
PANHANDLE LUMBER CO.   LUMBER
FRED TRUMBULL   ATTORNEY
IONE STATE BANK   BANK
IONE STEAM LAUNDRY   LDY
IRL HIGGS   BEER PARLOR
VERNE HAMBROOK   TRANSFER-
S.Q.DEAN   GROCERIES-DGS
BEN ENGSTROM   BLACKSMITH
SERVICE GARAGE   GARAGE
G.E.WIDGER   SHOW
GEO BROWN   SERVICE STATION
MRS MOORE   COFFEE SHOP
EA LOCKE   PAINTER
B.W.GARSKE   DYGDS-CONTRACTO
FURGANS   GROCERIES-FEED
O.L.SOADE   RESTAURANT
E.TRACKSTON   NEWS STAND
E.F.KIENITZ   DRY CLEANERS
IONE HOTEL   HOTEL
JESSIE NASH.TELEPHONE CO.
IONE HOSPITAL
H.S.ANDERSON   GROCERIES-MEAT
A MATHESON   DENTIST
S.H.STEVENS   ROOMS
A.J.WHITE. AGENT   CM3PP&P
T.GALLAGHER   GROCERIES-OIL
   LORNE REED   SAWMILL OPR
   JONATHAN REED   TRUCK OPERATOR

                  43

LIST OF BUSINESS MEN SIGNING THE
MC COY PETITION. 5-5-34

R.HALE   HALES DRYGDS
S.W.BLAZIER   GROCERIES-HDWE
W.S.CULVER   POOL HALL
IONE BAKERY   BAKERY
T.M.MC CARTHY   PENDOREILLE HOTEL
MRS A MOORE   COFFEE SHOP
F.W.GARSKE   DRYGDS & CONTACRTO
ANDY FOR   BARBER
LORNE REED   SAWMILL OPERATOR
JESSIE NASH   TELEPHONE
E.A.LOCKE   PAINTER
VERNE HAMBROOK   TRANSFER
SAM HALL   SUP'T PANHANDLE LBR CO
T.GALLAGHER   GROCERIES-OIL
FRED TRUMBULL   ATTORNEY
JOHN E MC COY   POSTS POLES
JOHN MC INTYRE   IONE HOTEL
G.E.WIDGER   SHOW
IRL HIGGS   BEER PARLOR
A.A.SHACKLETON   SERVICE GARAGE
E.M.BEARDSLEY   GROCERIES-FEED
S.H.STEVENS   ROOMS-VICKERMAN HDWE
GEO BROWN   SERVICE STATION
JONATHAN REED   TRUCK OPERATOR
MATT CLEARY   CLEARYS CAFE.

Ione Congregational Church, still in business today with
little change. This Photo was taken prior to 1912, because
the school was built that year and would be visible on the
left. Note present Highway 31, then just a mud track. Two
people, man and woman, are wading through the mud from
the church. Store front across Highway is the Ione Record,
long defunct newspaper.

Above, Author in 1927. The tall one is my dad who died June 5th, 1932, on Huckleberry Mountain, while building us a new house and was buried in an unmarked grave.

Right Top. Cars then were designed for posing kids for photos. Left to right, the author, younger brother Arnold, and oldest brother Raymond. Probably summer of 1931.

Bottom Right.. Not sure of date or names. Probably Betty True, my aunt, my brother Ray, and me. Probably Huckleberry Mountain, about 1930. Shows why we needed the Saturday night baths. Note chickens sharing the mud hole, in rear.

Above.. Then there were four, we now had sister Effie. About 1935. Dog is Snoose, (Because he looked at you, grinned, and sneezed). The rope off the front bumper suspends a pig carcass from a tree limb. The shadow in the foreground is mom with her Kodak box brownie camera.

Right Huckleberry Mountain School and student body, in 1932. Left to right, Front row, MacAuthur twins Bill and Phil, with author between, and Gracie MacAurthur. Middle row, Betty True. Rear, Dora, Dick, and Frank True, (my aunts and uncles), and Ronnie MacAurthur.

Above.. The three Lewis Boys and half sister Effie Alldredge, in winter attire, and the two family dogs. I can't remember the big ones name.. About 1935.

Right The Panhandle Mille, Ione's reason for existence, was built when the railroad came in, about 1909, and was junked out by Alaska Junk about 1937. Of many mills built on the river north of Newport, it was the largest. Many of the smaller houses in town were constructed as mill houses for workers, as was the Hotel Pend Oreille on Central and Main streets. They also furnished electricity for the town.

Above Ione Ferry. Crossed the Pend Oreille River at the foot of Main Street, from the present park. It was replaced by the bridge in early 1930s

Right Top.. Highway 31 (Now) looking north across the dam to Ione, with Cement mountain in the background, about 1930. Road was still dirt and snow was not yet plowed.

Right Bottom.. Same road looking north across Cedar Creek bridge through now defunct town of Cement. Road was so narrow, one vehicle (Usually Wagons) would have to pull off to let another pass. Bridge was wood, with heavy planks laid lengthwise where wheels would run.

Above Men on handcar in front of Ione depot.
Building still exists, but has been moved across
Railroad Street at Main.

Top Right Group of men in front of Hotel Pend
Oreille on Ione's Main street. Bun Hambrook is only
one identified. Probably early 1930s.

Bottom Right. Main Street of Ione, about same
time. Note dirt streets and wooden sidewalks.
Otherwise not much changed except there are many
fewer buildings.

Narrow gauge Electric trains ran through much of the
lumber yard that extended from the mill north to the alley
south of Blackwell Street.

Horses and wagons with steel clad wheels were used in parts of yard with no rails. Driver is Bun Hambrook.

Sophmore Class, Spring of 1942. Classes were shrinking with people leaving area and others enlisting in service. Author, tallest one, in center of rear row.

CHAPTER XIII

Unfortunately, memories come in both good and bad. One of the worst was the time I came home and found Doctor Canning's car parked in front of the house and my mother crying when I went inside. Ole had had a massive heart attack Now it would probably have a more high tech name, but it was just a bad heart attack then.

The prognosis was not good. The Doctor said if he would survive for twenty four hours, and not have another one, he might stand a chance. I'm sure my mother could see herself burying her second husband at the age of about thirty. The bad part is that Doc Canning's prediction came true, he did have another one and did not survive it. The good part was that it happened in Portland, and about thirty years later. The sad part was that he worked his tail off all his life in construction, and couldn't wait to reach sixty two so he could retire. He lived for less than a year after retiring.

Another bad part of the first one was the fact that this left my mother with four kids, I was the oldest at less than ten, and an invalid husband to support until he recovered enough to work. I suspect that this was part of the reason she ended up working so much for Doc Canning. He had a way of caring for his flock in other than medical ways. More than one would have sworn he could walk on water, despite his wooden leg. I have heard varying stories, from he lost a foot in France during WW1, to he lost it in a farm accident. I always liked the former, it went more with his image in Ione.

The mill had cement floors in many areas and used lumber wagons weighing hundreds of pounds when loaded, with steel wheels, and there was a narrow gauge railroad running throughout the yards. I don't remember a name, but a young local fell and his leg was crushed when run over by one of these. Most opined that they should just cut it off. Doc Canning disagreed, I'm sure because of his life with only one leg, and refused to do so. I guess it took many months of reconstruction work, but he did save the leg, even with the limited facilities available at the time.

As I mentioned before, my grandparents still lived on Huckleberry Mountain. I had acquired new aunts at the same rate as brothers. My aunt Betty was the nine days older than me, my aunt Millie was two years younger, the same age as my older brother, and my aunt Beulah was the same age as my younger brother, or four years my junior. We still spent many happy hours visiting with them and running the mountain, as well as some more productive ones.

The growing season was short, even shorter than Ione's, because of the elevation. Peas, Green Beans, Radishes, and Leaf Lettuce were possible, but because of longer growing times, and being attractions to the deer, Carrots and Potatoes were iffy, but were planted anyway. Actually, carrots the size of your little finger, with the dirt wiped off on your pants leg, are the sweetest. There were plenty of wild Strawberries all around the area but they were very small and it took a lot to be enough to do anything. For several years after the Tiger Hill burn, mushrooms were plentiful, and we ate them fixed every way possible. Fried in butter was my favorite.

There was no shortage of dandelions though. When they arrived as soon as the snow left, we ate a lot of them for salads. You take the young leaves and strip the center vein out and you have lettuce. Mom said they were high in vitamins. She was big on vitamins. I'm sure it was in part because of her work with Doctor Canning, and with her care of a lot of people who were suffering from pneumonia, probably partially diet related.

She used to feed us a teaspoonful of Cod Liver oil daily in the winter. Usually she mixed it in orange juice when we could afford it. To this day I can't drink orange juice without a shudder. She also favored Ex-Lax and Nature's Remedy.

I'm not sure of the purpose of Nature's Remedy, but it looked like a green aspirin, as if made of Alf-Alfa like rabbit pellets. They had the same inclination of sticking to the tongue as an aspirin. Nothing else is as bitter and as hard to remove the taste from the mouth as Natures Remedy. My most vivid memory of Nature's Remedy was when my youngest brother insisted on trying some chewing tobacco we had liberated from the lumber yard. It tasted so good he couldn't bring himself to spit out the juice. Maybe the green color he turned is what led my mother to think of the green pills, but she made me chew up a couple of the bitter things as punishment. Not sure of the connection, but it got my attention.

It's funny that a recent TV show should remind me of my mother's method of last resort when the X-Lax didn't live up to her expectations. On one of the talk shows an actress was talking about having discovered colonics and how great they were. My mother discovered them way back in the thirties. Only they were just called enemas then and we didn't consider them very great. The red rubber bag hung threateningly on the back of a door in our house, ready for action at all times. She kept the fever thermometer just as handy and any rise in temperature was certain to be sufficient cause for one treatment. They must have been great though as the mere mention of maybe needing one would cure most any health problem. The illness would disappear magically.

Huckleberries were a cash crop even then. The better picking patches were in the area above the present Meadow Lake. This was about a three mile walk from the grandparent's house. We would walk up to the patch with our lunch, spend all day picking, and then walk back home. If the picking was good, we could pick about two gallons each. The next day we would walk the five miles to town and go door to door in Ione and sell them. I think they usually sold for around fifty cents a gallon.

I also have memories of huckleberry picking, some good and some not so good. I think I also mentioned that we went barefoot as soon as the snow melted. We were picking one day when my uncle Dick stepped into a bees nest. Some bees, I'm not sure which kind, built their nests in holes in the ground, usually under piles of brush, and usually impossible to see. He got mad when they stung him, and started throwing things at the nest and got stung again which made him even madder. The rest of us thought it funny, so I guess this was a good memory for us, probably not so good a memory for him.

Another time, I was picking on one side of a clump of bushes and most of the others were on the other side. I heard a noise in the bushes and thought it was Uncle Dick. When he wouldn't answer, I started to push my way through the brush and came face to face with a fair sized black bear. Again, I don't know if the bear considered this a good time or a bad time, but there was no doubt about my point of view. I didn't even think it near as funny as some of my Aunts did. They spent the whole trip home discussing whether the bear or I was running the fastest. Some jibes, probably not suitable for a family paper, about why he couldn't get any traction while running behind me was why he couldn't catch up with me

One memory that I'm quite sure would fit in the not good category was from the other end of the enterprise. We were going door to door with our buckets of berries, buckets being empty lard pails. When you carry them, berries tend to settle in the pail and we had carried them for about eight miles by the time we reached Ione. I knocked on one door and it was answered by a rather severe looking lady. She told me she didn't think there was a gallon of berries in my pail.

I was privileged to stand and watch her put the berries into a quart jar and smash them down until they were mostly just juice and then empty the jar into a pan. When they didn't fill the fourth jar completely she accused me of trying to cheat her. I then got to watch her pour the squashed berries back into my bucket, just before she showed me the door. I found out later she was the wife of the Brown who owned Brown's Shell on the corner of the highway and Main Street.

What's an eleven year old boy to do. Probably scarred me for life. I tried several sales jobs over the years, but have never been able to sell anything since. At least that's my excuse and I'm sticking to it.

CHAPTER XIV

By 1937, things were improving. Ole had recovered from his attack and was working some. My mother was working part time. There was enough money in the house that we kids were given an allowance. Twenty five cents a week. Of course we were to buy our school supplies like pencils and paper out of it. I do seem to remember though, it only lasted a couple weeks, I'm not sure why it was cancelled, and I'm not sure I was too unhappy to see it go because it wasn't too profitable from our end.

We now had two cows, by dint of not eating a heifer calf. Bulls never made it through a winter. I say winter as that was the time for butchering. Winter when it is cold enough to preserve the meat by freezing it. We still had no refrigeration. But we sold both milk and butter churned from the cream.

My mother decided she would get into the egg business also. The folks built a new chicken house, all out of shiny new lumber, with a high fence around it that was guaranteed to keep out the skunks and other varmints, in the woods behind the house. She ordered some baby chicks from either a Sears or Montgomery Wards catalog and they came in parcel post. We previously had a few chickens running loose that were a mixture of Rhode Island Reds and Barred Rocks, but they were for eating. She ordered White Leghorns because they were supposed to lay more eggs. They also were all supposed to be pullets. I could never understand how they could be sure when they just little yellow balls of fuzz.

The chickens were several months old, I'm not sure just how old, but running around and flying over the fence on occasion until their wing feathers were clipped. Then they started acting funny. First a few and then more and more. They would run around with their necks drooping almost as much as the one my mother had shot when we lived on the hill.

Mom called the county agent and he came out and told her the chickens had limber neck. When she questioned, he caught a hen, held its body under his left arm, and with a quick twist with his right, removed it's head. He held the chicken's head out to mom and explained what was the matter as he held the neck with the blood spurting out, with his left hand. Of course all of us kids standing around watching considered it a good show. Mom didn't.

He then told mom that there was no cure, that they could not be eaten, and would all have to be destroyed. He then went on to tell her that the chicken house would have to be burned, and that no chickens could be raised in the same location as the disease was in the dirt and would be for years, and there was no way to get rid of it. So ended my mothers attempt at starting an egg raising empire.

Mom always had to name all of the animals, which sometimes led to bad feelings when it came time to eat them. The cows all had names. Even some of the chickens had names. I don't remember them, but I do remember Lulubelle, the pig. She lived in a lean-to house on the side of the barn, with a small run out back. She had at least one litter of pigs, before she became almost impossible to keep contained. She was huge, and had a rather bad disposition, and could walk through almost any fence put up to contain her.

It was about Thanksgiving time when Ole decided her time had arrived. There was a large tree in the yard, about midway between the house and the barn. He asked a young neighbor, I think it was Ronnie McArthur but I'm not sure, to help in exchange for some of the meat. They built a fire next to the tree, around a fifty five gallon barrel, where it was under a large limb. They filled it with water, and kept the fire stoked all day and over one night until the water was boiling. Ole brought out the twenty two, the old Remington pump with a long hex barrel and a tube magazine underneath. This was a twenty two WRF, a 22 caliber, but the shell was longer and it had more power than the standard. A lot more power than the 22 shorts we kids put through it.

Ronnie, or whoever, said he had shot game before but never a pig and asked if he could do it. I think Ole was somewhat relieved as he had been feeding her for over a year so he said yes. Ronnie got in the pen and when Lulubelle started toward him he shot her between the eyes. The bullet just glanced off and in to the wall of the barn. I don't remember it making any ricochet noise like they always do on TV. This made her madder than heck for some reason. Ronnie scrabbled out over the fence just before the pig went right through it under him. She was going for blood and didn't appear to care whose it was.

Eventually the pig lost and was dragged up to the tree with the car. A rope was fastened to a stick, sharpened on each end and run through the Achilles tendon and then passed through a pulley on the limb. She was hoisted up by the car and lowered down into the barrel of hot water, briefly, to loosen the hair. she was then hoisted back up and all the loosened hair scraped off. The meat was left hanging in the tree where it remained frozen for a good portion of the winter until it was eaten.

Under this tree was also the wood cutting place. The tree was large and kept the area under it fairly clear of snow most of the winter, so the wood saw was set up here. The saw was an approximately thirty inch circular saw mounted on a wooden frame, powered by a belt running off the rear wheel of the car. Worked great as long as the car could be started in the cold weather, which was sometimes iffy. The usual way to start a car, most any car, in winter was to pour hot water into the radiator that had been drained to keep it from freezing overnight and hope you could get it running before the water froze.

Ole sometimes worked for Loren Reed cutting wood on a similar saw, except it was powered by a Diesel tractor. The tractor had a small gas motor that was supposed to turn the diesel over to get it running. I seem to remember it also took a lot of four letter words to get it started in winter. I believe the tractor is the one still sitting in the Reed pasture off Mc Innis street.

The twenty two WRF was the rifle that we kids wandered the whole area with. I'm not sure how old I was the first time I took it out, but I know it was by the time I was in the sixth grade. It was a different time. Course we could never afford the WRF shells. 22 shorts would almost fit crosswise in the chamber, and were too short to work in the magazine, so we had to load them one at a time, but they were only thirty five cents a box as apposed to somewhere around a dollar and a half for the WRF. Actually I got quite good with the gun, even surprising myself on occasion.

We also had another rifle, but it was understood that we kids didn't mess with it. It also was a Remington with an even longer and thicker hex barrel with a white bone front sight and an open rear sight. It was a much larger caliber, and lived on a pair of nails on the living room wall. It was a forty sixty five caliber, that I guess was sort of an oddity. Doc Canning always coveted it, and when we moved from the area my mother arranged for it to be delivered to him much to my chagrin.

We never touched it, except. The folks were all gone one day and curiosity got the better of me. I placed a tin can in the field below the house, sat on the top step of the porch at the back door, and aimed carefully. The gun was heavy, the noise scared me, and the smoke from the black powder obliterated my view of the can so I had to walk down and check for accuracy. I missed the can by about three feet.

Ole smelled the gun powder when they came home shortly afterwards. He never said anything to me, but that evening he took the rifle down, smelled the barrel, and announced he thought it needed cleaning and it was about time I learned how to clean a rifle.

CHAPTER XV

The fall of 37, I moved across the hall. At school that is. Third, fourth, and fifth grades shared two rooms, with fourth more or less permanently divided in half. Sixth, Seventh, and eighth, shared two rooms with classes moving back and forth so one class would be taught in each room, with the odd class divided and having study hall.

They were also different in that they had the schools two male teachers. Unfortunately they were not different in their position on the dam kids. We still ran the gauntlet. Different in that I had a girl named Ida Calhoun, who did me a favor and carried it back to the teacher. She claimed she told him I was being picked on, but he only saw it as I was fighting on the way home. He wouldn't believe it was only when I couldn't run fast enough to get out of it

He would keep us after school for fighting, then let both sides of the fight go at the same time so I would have to defend myself again to get out if town to go home. The guys would blame me for telling the teacher and getting them in trouble and the fight would be on. Ida would tell the teacher again the next day, and I was in trouble again for fighting.

After several of these, with threats getting more and more dire, the teacher decided to use corporal punishment. I don't remember it applying to the others, but he made me bend over his desk and took out his favorite persuader. It was a piece of rubber hose about two feet long, which he applied liberally to my backsides, at the front of the room in front of the class.

It left me sore enough to not move easily, but I toughed it out for a couple of days until my brother saw my bruises that went from my belt to the middle of my thighs. He told mom. She made me drop my pants and show her. She took me to school and made me drop my pants and show the teacher. She then informed the teacher that if he ever touched another of her kids she would come to school with a baseball bat and use it on him. My mother never used much profanity so it surprised me when she several times used references to his ancestry that inferred his mother was of the canine family. He must have believed her as life got a little easier. In fact I never saw the hose used on anyone else again either.

It was not too long after this that the folks bought a house in town. It was a store front on the south east corner of South Central and Blackwell, now occupied by the Food Court Store, and had an apartment behind. They partitioned the back half of the storefront into two bedrooms and retained the storefront, as it rented as a polling place each election. I think the rental was about fifteen dollars, once or twice a year, which meant it was worth more for a rental than for bedrooms. My bedroom was about where the store's lunch meats and cheese are now kept. The house was on a quarter block of land, and I believe they paid fifteen hundred dollars for the whole thing. About half of it became the family garden. I was privileged to learn about a number two shovel and some of its uses there.

It had a wood shed out behind at the alley, with an outhouse along side, and a garage on the back corner on Central. Zelva Boyer lived in the center house across the street from us. She was what the kids would refer to today as a hottie. She was the only one in my class younger than I, by I think about one or two months, throughout my years in Ione School. I always had a crush on her, but I didn't think she reciprocated, so I never mentioned it nor did she.

By that time the town had installed their diesel generator, to furnish electricity formerly furnished by the mill, just down the street where the present fire station is located. We could hear it running day and night. Actually I am sure it was probably less noisy than the mill it replaced would have been, but I hadn't lived close to the mill when it was operating.

By this time the lumber yard was mostly vacant so we had a large empty field out behind. The half of the block between us and the highway was owned by the Hambrooks, who owned the transfer and storage business in town. Donna Hambrook Bell is one of only half a dozen people that I have found who are still around from this era. Most of these have mentioned that they didn't know me, they knew my younger brother, thereby inferring they are younger than I. Of course this makes my doing this column easier as there is no one around able to question my facts, at least without stating their age.

I'm not sure of the year, but somewhere around 1937 or 1938 Harold Matsuta joined the class. He was a nephew of Mr. Terroka who owned the laundry and cleaners. He had completed high school in Japan before the Terrokas brought him to the states. He started with first grade and spent about two or three years catching up with us in either the sixth or seventh grade and then stayed with our class through high school.

Mr. Terroka told us he brought Harold over here because the war was threatening and Japan had universal conscription so he would have been drafted into the Japanese army. Somewhat later he also told us that the US would undoubtedly win in the war, but that it was going to take a lot longer than everyone here thought. Of course us guys knew that we would just send a couple of battle ships over there and they would quit. I'm sure most of our elders had similar opinions. I digress, that was three or four years later.

Not too long after we moved to town, I began delivering the Spokane Chronicle, the evening paper. I would go to Shackleton's Texaco, the Greyhound depot, and get my papers off the bus when it came in in the evening. It was late enough that it would be full dark and very cold when they arrived in the winter time. I sit here tonight and look out at today's snowfall and remember how cold and wet I used to get, slogging through the snow with my load of papers. It was actually worse when the snow started to thaw and the ruts would be full of very cold water.

Most roads around the edge of town were not plowed on a regular basis, and one walked in the ruts made by the few cars that were out. Many paths to houses were just paths made by people walking them and never shoveled. They were hard to find in the dark The paper route included houses from out what is now labeled Greenhouse Road, to across Cedar Creek, and used to take about two hours. Someone else had the route across the dam. I think the paper used to cost a nickel, or one dollar and fifty cents a month, and my cut was twenty five or fifty cents, but I'm not sure. Somewhere around a penny per paper per night. In the summer time it was nice as it was daylight and warm and I could use my bike, but my memory is of a lot more winter than summer.

At the end of the school each year we would have

a picnic at one of the local lakes, either Sullivan Lake or one of the Little Pend Oreille Lakes. One year, I'm again not sure exactly but I was somewhere around grade six, we went to Sullivan Lake. It was not a very warm day and we were on the north end of the lake. There was enough wind from the south end to make whitecap waves on the lake, and it was chilly but nice enough that many of us were playing in the edge of the water.

Another of the recession recovery programs was the Civilian Conservation Corps, CCC, about like the present Job Corps, except to my knowledge only forest oriented. They wore uniforms like the army, and one of the camps was located just off the north end of Sullivan Lake. These were youths in their upper teens, and one of them came down to the lake carrying a small row boat. He launched the boat and got in and proceeded to row out a couple hundred feet. I'm not sure what happened, but suddenly the boat was upside down and the CCC was on top of it. Had he stayed still the wind would probably have blown him back to shore, but he stood up on the boat and dove into the water. He couldn't swim, and drowned in front of the group of kids. Great ending to a happy day.

CHAPTER XVI

It was about 1938 that the Forest Service bought out all of the few families left on Huckleberry Mountain. On this side of the mountain that was my grandparents and the Mc Arthur family, and maybe a couple families who didn't actually live on their places. I think there were also a couple of families over the hill in Stevens County, but that is based on recent discoveries, as that was foreign country to us at the time. I have heard it referred to as the "Re-Settlement Program," but at the time all I heard was the "Re-Forestation Project."

In my grandparents case, they were bought out and helped to move to a dairy farm at Roy, a small crossroads west of Portland, Oregon. As I understood it, the government made a down payment on an operating farm. Problems arose because my grandfather wasn't a farmer. By the early forties they had given up on the farm and moved to Portland and most of the family was working in the shipyards.

The Forest Service came in and bulldozed down all of the structures on the mountain and then burned the piles. This totally ended an era. I have recently visited the area and have been able to locate where my grandparents house was and where the Huckleberry Mountain school was. All that is left of the school is a few bricks from the chimney and a mushroom shaped piece of cement that once held the flag pole in the ground. I understand the school house itself is now a residence that sits on the South West corner of

Seventh and Houghton in Ione.

At the place where my grandparents house was located I found a few rocks around a shallow hole left from the root cellar where the house sat and a few old cans and bottles on the creek bank left over from their garbage dump. About a half mile further south on their road at Jimmie Kinnette's place I found only the head of an old iron bed frame, nary a sign of the Model T Ford that used to sit in the barn, or the barn it sat in for that matter. Of the McArthur place or the place we originally lived, or the "new" house built for us by my grandparents, I can find not a trace.

Again I'm not sure of the exact date, but it was about this time that the infamous state sales tax was installed. It started as a penny on a dollar, but the state government fell in love with it so it like all things government, grew exponentially. At the beginning we had aluminum coins slightly bigger than a nickel, with a hole in the middle. They were three for a penny. During the war they became green plastic to save metal.

During the years the tokens disappeared as they couldn't keep up with the tax increases that became almost eight cents on a dollar. This would mean about one token for three cents today. This at the same time as the price of things taxed went up by a factor of about twenty for a tax increase of about one hundred sixty times.

This was also about the time Social Security came on the scene. I believe my first contributions were made in its second year, 1939.

They say that things bad come in threes. Also in 38, I moved to the seventh grade, and my half of the class was assigned seats in the eighth grade room. I drew a seat three or four from the front and along the inside wall. This room was ruled by the other man teacher in the school who was also the school principal. This was also the man who kicked my hind end all the way around the ball diamond, and the one who's hat I had knocked off with a snowball, so I really wasn't looking forward to being in his room.

Most of the students had forgiven my across the dam heritage. I'm not sure if it was because I now lived in town or because I was fairly large for my age and had managed to best a couple of the guys who had caught me. The teachers were not that quick to forgive.

I was sitting in my seat alongside the wall, supposedly studying, while the eighth grade students had a class on the window side of the room. I was reading a forbidden comic book, hidden inside my notebook. I failed to keep track of the teacher and he went to the rear of the room on the other side, where he could see my transgression. My first indication I was in trouble was a loud, "Crack," when a piece of chalk shattered on the wall beside my head. I looked around to see where it came from in time to dodge the eraser that followed it.

Not sure if I got the ultimate punishment came because I ducked and caused him to miss, or from the original infraction, but I was ordered to the front of the room where I was told to bend over and grab my ankles. The teacher then applied the paddle he had saved from his hazing days in college and kept in his desk. It was about thirty inches long, five inches wide, of three quarter inch plywood, with a number of holes drilled through it. Depending on their weight, about three swats would propel most any of the guys all the way across the room. Always in front of the class, the most embarrassing part. I wasn't the only one treated to this form of teaching, but think I received more than a proportionate number of lessons. Girls hadn't achieved equality yet so were exempt.

Fortunes must have been looking up because about this time I remember Ole was driving truck for the county, and I remember him coming home and saying that he had received a ten cent per hour raise. He went from four dollars and eighty cents a day to five dollars and sixty cents. Feeding a family of six. But a new, to us at least, car showed up in the garage. It was a thirty two Studebaker President, with a straight eight engine under a hood that protruded something like three and a half feet in front of the flat, vertical windshield. With a round thermometer, with glass on each side so you could read it from either the front or the rear, out on the front atop the chromed radiator mount.

It was an all black except for chrome trim, four door sedan, with extra space in the back so there were two jump seats that dropped down from the back of the front seat. There were lights and vases, up on both sides inside the back seat area and chrome S shaped trims on the outside. There was a leather covered trunk on a platform on the back that had leather straps to close it.

It was not only much larger than the old Chev, but was also much faster. On a trip to the fair at Cusick, Ole got her up to sixty miles an hour and everyone Ohed and Ahed. I'm sure the road was more of a limiting factor than the car itself, but at the time I wouldn't have thought of that.

Another of the few trips I remember taking in the Studebaker was when the first airplane I ever saw came to town. It was an old biplane, probably left over from World War One, that circled over town a few times and then landed in a farmers field about five miles south on LeClerc Road. He was offering rides. Fifteen minutes for five bucks, with two people at a time jammed into the front open cockpit.

Take offs and landings were accompanied by lots of dust and smoke, and of course plenty of exciting noise. Five dollars was out of question for us, but I did get up near enough to touch the plane and smell the caster oil used for lubrication of the old engines. It was later that I learned that pilots had to use care in where they left their planes unattended as this smell attracted cows. They would literally eat the fabric right off the airplane.

CHAPTER XVII

On the corner, across the unpaved stub end of North Central Street from the school, in a building not much larger than a one car garage was the Ione Town Hall. In a smaller building behind it was the fire department. The fire equipment consisted of a hand hose cart, with a rail for pumping on each side, some hose coiled along side, and a tongue on front for a couple of men to pull. North of the town hall was the bell tower. It was probably ten feet square on the ground, and tapered up to about fifteen feet tall, with a bell on top. The bell now is mounted at ground level in the town park. A barbwire fence chopped the road off about a half block back, with a style over it giving access to, I believe the Stecker's field behind.

Not sure of the occasion, but there were a number of men waiting around outside of the town hall on the day I remember. I think it must have had something to do with one the programs of the Roosevelt era, such as WPA or NRA. I left school to go home and was stopped by a boy named Danny Ferguson, one of my old opponents. I don't think anyone was injured very badly, but we rolled around in the dust of the unpaved street, with an occasional blow being landed, for what seemed an eternity, much to the entertainment of the gathering of men by the town hall, and the gathering of kids on the edge of the school ball field across the street.

One of his friends, I think Danny lived on the corner across from the church and Roy Madsen his friend in arms lived somewhere close. When he tried to come to his aid the men wouldn't let him. Roy's dad was town marshal, not sure if it was at that time, and not sure that had anything to do with it.

The school principal came out and tried to break it up and the men told him we were off the school grounds and it was none of his business. He left, but I was sure I would pay the next day. Some how, I ended up sitting on top of Danny and was willing to pound his head into the ground, but the men wouldn't let me do that either, as it wouldn't be fair. I wasn't interested in fair at that time, but he was ready to quit so we did. I don't remember having any more fights after that one. Guess I had outgrown it, or just got bigger than the opponents maybe.

A problem with being on the second floor at school was the fact that one could see too much outside. As I mentioned earlier, we kids wandered the countryside, usually with rifle in hand. One of the favorites was Cement Mountain. It loomed up right outside our windows from either of the sixth through eighth grade rooms and was hard to disregard when the weather was good
.There were lots of squirrels and a few grouse on the mountain and we usually had our twenty-twos. I don't think I really liked eating squirrels, sort of like cooking a rat, but we built fires and cooked them anyway. They were tough and stingy and the amount of meat not worth the effort. Grouse wasn't a great deal better, but a guy's got to maintain face with the rest of the boys, so I gnawed my way through several of each.

We climbed all over the mountain numerous times. The cliffs at the east side were, in our eyes at least rather dangerous, so were especially interesting.

A couple of grandsons, age about twelve, were recently visiting and complained of nothing to do. I suggested they could climb the mountain, there being no chance of getting lost as they could see the house all the way up. The comment of one was, "Isn't there a road going up there so you could drive us up?"

It was about this time that the sidewalks on main street were replaced, another WPA project I believe. They had been boardwalks from the beginning of Ione, with cracks that gobbled up coins at any opportunity. We would always keep an eye on the cracks as we walked and occasionally would find a coin shining up from below and spend hours rescuing it. When they were tearing the old walks up we patrolled the dirt, but with the tight economy I am sure that the tearer-uppers didn't miss too many coins as they were probably working for less than five dollars a day.

Harold Matsuta, the Japanese student who had joined us in sixth or seventh grade was much older than us. Old enough, eighteen I think, that he could play the pinball machines. They used nickels and were in all of the taverns, and even Moes Ice Cream Shop where we hung out had a couple. In fact he had gambling problem I fear.

We found a cigar box full of tokens from a defunct pool hall when one portion of the walk was lifted along by Jane's drug store east from fourth. I guess the workers must have decided they were worthless. They were made of aluminum and the same size as the coins they represented, nickels, dimes, quarters, and halves.

We sold the nickels to Harold, two for a nickel I think. He proceeded to feed them into the pinball machines in a couple of places. He got caught by the owners and was forced to buy back all of the slugs from the machines. Maybe we felt bad about it, but I don't recall ever offering to buy them back from him. Probably be worth a lot more than face now, but not then. Over my lifetime I have probably done away with a fortune in collectables, just before they became collectables.

It was about this time that we became aware of the old Hotel Pend Oreille, now labeled the Coyner building. It was larger then than it is now, extending all the way back to the alley, and had a single story roof over the sidewalk. It had back porches at each level and an open framework up the back. The front entry was into the lobby on your left and there was a restaurant to the right, and the kitchen toward the rear. The stairs up in between were just as steep as now, but I remember them being wider and open sided. The two upper floors were rooms with a bath or two on each floor. Another stairs went down at the back to what was the kitchen area.

It was all locked up, on the ground floor, but it was simple to climb up the back to the second where it wasn't. We would climb out on to the roof over the street or make weird noises from the windows up above when any kids we knew came by. I'm not sure it didn't scare us as much as the kids outside who were the targets. We would move around inside the windows so they could catch flashes of us in the too dim light from the street lights or anything we could think of to attract their attention.

Several times we were called to the attention of the Town Marshall, but he didn't stand a chance. We could move between floors too many ways, and quietly as we knew which boards squeaked, so he couldn't slip up on us. To my knowledge, no one ever intentionally caused any damage. But hopefully the statutes of limitations on trespass have run out.

Again I'm not sure if it belongs here or not, but I just had another flash of memory. Another practice that would probably bring us the disapproval of the local officers. A car would be chained, in winter of course, and one or two ropes would be stretched out from the rear. Guys on skis would hang on to the ropes and be pulled along. The picture I received is of the car proceeding out Sullivan Lake road, and skiers being on each side of the road, and the snow being deep enough that the fence posts were mere nubs, and did not interfere with the ropes.

CHAPTER XIIX

By the eighth grade things had quieted down somewhat, or at least other than an occasional session with the teachers favorite paddle, I have few memories. Not sure if I developed calluses or I just got used to them.

I had decided to save up my earnings from the paper route and spend the summer after graduation at my grandparents farm in Oregon. I watched my account at Betty's Ione State Bank grow, slowly. I'm sure the amount needed was probably under twenty dollars, but that represented several months income from the paper route. Toward the end of the year I had to find someone to take over the route. Fairly easy during the good weather of spring.

Time drug on, but finally I was declared competent to climb the final flight of stairs. Next fall I would be in high school.

The trip to Oregon involved my boarding the local Greyhound bus at Shackleton's garage for the trip to Spokane, where I would transfer to the bus to Portland, where I would again change busses and proceed to Cornelius, Oregon, some thirty five miles to the west. I had in mind a slightly different itinerary. I had heard the Oscarson family had moved to Ione, Oregon, but I wasn't sure they had or to where in the area they might live. I had lost a good friend with their departure, so I decided I would stop and look him up on the way down.

At Spokane I found out how I could go to Ione, Oregon, and they arranged for me to take a stopover. Actually I found out that you couldn't get there by bus, I would have to get off the bus at, I think, a cross roads called Heppner Junction, and from there I would need to hitchhike about thirty mile south on a very secondary road. Even the good roads were less than today's secondary roads, so this one was probably gravel and a lot less than heavily traveled.

I was doing fine until I reached Ione, Oregon, a town no larger than Ione, Washington, and could find no one who had even heard of the Oscarsons. Since telephones were still a luxury item it wasn't just a matter of checking a phone book. Also, being new people, they probably would not be known by everyone.

I had departed from Ione on the morning bus, but by the time I gave up it was getting dark, and hitchhiking only works when there are cars. It took me until well into the night to get back to the junction where there was no actual bus station. I asked some of the locals and found out there was not another bus to Portland until the next afternoon.

I was thirteen years old and owned the world, but it was a long time until the next bus and cold in spite the fact it was spring. It was also getting hungry. I had never walked into a restaurant and ordered a meal, and there probably wasn't a restaurant there anyway. Also I wasn't sure what a meal would cost, and if I had money enough to pay for one.

All good things come to an end. I finally made Portland and had no trouble catching the bus to Cornelius where I was dropped in front of a grocery store. Actually the store, a feed store, and a gas station across the highway was Cornelius. It was getting close to dark again and I didn't have a clue. The station was the least daunting, so I tried it first, but they had never heard of the True family. I re-crossed the highway and got lucky at the store. A boy who was working there went to the same high school in Hillsboro as my aunts.

I was told, I should take the highway that went out beside the store. The family lived out about ten miles by the even smaller town of Roy, although their address was Cornelius. Ten miles, and it was nearing dark. Again I got lucky, people were friendly. The first car to pass stopped and they also knew the family. They hauled me to their house, made a phone call, and one of my uncles came to pick me up. I had made it to within a mile of their farm.

Everyone was surprised to see me, as they hadn't received the letter announcing my arrival yet. There was a lot of excited milling around of all of the aunts and it was not long before the arrival of some of my cousins who lived about a mile down the road. One of my grandmothers first questions was, "When did you eat last?" It didn't take her long to remedy the deficit.

I learned one lesson that summer. I was never cut out to be a farmer. My granddad asked if I would like to work while I was there. I agreed and he said he would pay me a dollar and a half a day. The days began at daylight, somewhere around five, when we would get up and milk a herd of about thirty cows, separate the cream, and after cooling put the whole out for the milk truck from the creamery to pick up. Next we went in for breakfast.

By the time we finished eating, the dew would have evaporated so we could hit the fields. Depending on what we were doing, we had lunch, either delivered to the field or at the house, and went back to work. We worked until about five, when we had another date with the cows. The second lesson was that all cows are alike. I hated these cows as much as those at home. After a heavy dinner we went back to the fields and worked by the lights on the equipment until the dew settled again, usually about ten or eleven at night. Made five in the morning come awfully quick.

Again there were good things and bad things; I wore out a pair of shoes. The leather sides not the soles, in about ten days of walking ahead of and feeding the combine while harvesting the Hairy Vetch. This was a plant resembling alfalfa that was grown for seed, used for ground cover back in the dust bowl of the Midwest.

During pea harvest we spent a lot of time sitting in the car, waiting for trucks that were hauling to the cannery, 24 hours a day. It was done on a Co-op basis and we worked one farm then moved on to the neighbor the next day, or night on many occasions. The next door neighbor to my grandparents farm made grape wine. When we were working his peas, I learned that the sweet taste was really a trap. One night they convinced me it would keep me warm. I went to sleep and when they woke me to load the next truck, I had a terrific head ache and a vow of never again.

Haying was one of my least favorites. The hay wagon was pulled by the tractor while we pitched the dried hay on to it. The part of the hay that didn't go down your neck. The hay had its share of cheat grass that has seeds like porcupine quills. Sharp on one end with barbs that not only keep it from backing out, but actually make it work in deeper, especially in your sox, just at the top of your shoes, where the shoes keep pushing them in to your ankles.

The only good part was one of the neighbor girls, a big gal who was slightly older than I. She would come by and take my place on the hay operation, in her swimming suit which no one could fathom, while I took her younger sister swimming in the swimming hole in the local creek. Her sister was a very cute little red head named Helen Weller, actually my age, and I didn't mind baby sitting at all. I don't remember the older sisters name though.

I saw some of the reasons for my granddad not being the most successful at farming. For one he kept a pair of very beautiful dapple gray horses, huge things, whose only use was pulling the hay up in to the hay loft after it was harvested by the tractor, and pulling the cultivator through the corn field a couple of days a year. They were fed like they were really working, but probably didn't work over ten days a year and then not very hard. We tried to ride them on occasion, but it was like sitting atop a table as they were so wide and fat. A total waste of money, but he was very proud of them.

Then there was Portland. His favorite part of farming was running in to Portland for a part for some piece of equipment that had broken down. I sometimes suspected he may have sabotaged the equipment just for the excuse. I made a couple of these trips with him. The thirty mile trip took all afternoon, as a necessary part of every trip was a stop at either or both of Portland's burlesque theaters, The Star, and The Gayety. They were not high class theater, so could have been a liberal education for me, but at thirteen I didn't understand most of the jokes and innuendos.

I was not too unhappy to see the summer become history. By the end of the summer I had accumulated enough money to pay for my ticket home, but not much more. Several of the family took me to Portland and put me on the bus in the middle of the night, and I had learned my lesson, I stayed on it until it got to Spokane. I arrived back home, mostly broke, in time to begin my daily climb to the third floor of the school. I was now a high schooler.

My finances improved almost immediately. During the summer, Mr. Johnson, the school janitor suffered a heart attack. In order to lighten his load, I was offered a job as his assistant. It began as temporary with pay on an hourly basis, but they soon gave me my own key and put me on the school payroll. I worked two or three hours each evening after school. My job was sweeping out the whole school, dumping the waste baskets in the classrooms, and generally straightening up the rooms. My pay after I got on the payroll would be $30 per month.

The having my own key part led to several interesting discoveries. The classrooms all had doors with small windows, but many of them had been covered by the teachers for one reason or another. The teachers of the lower grades were barely out of college, I think two years college was all that was required then, so they were not much older than some of the older high school boys. Just say that in a few instances, upon opening a door I would discover things that would lead me to close it again and do another room before returning. The older boys were much larger than I.

The job almost made turning out for sports impossible, which didn't make me too popular because of the shortage of boys. I did turn out for football, briefly. Six man football that is. I was right end. The first game, against Metaline Falls, I rushed full speed, and the opposing end just laid down. I fell over him and plowed up the turf with my nose. Not sure now, whether the reason I quit was the job or the nose in the dirt.

CHAPTER XIX

For seven years I had watched the high school guys go up the stairs. Actually some of us had sneaked up and checked it out in spite of the threats. Now it was my turn. The first day we met in the study hall, the middle room that took up over half of the north side of the building. The seats in study hall, old fashioned desks with cast iron filigree sides, a fold up seat, and the wooden tops with a groove for pencils at the top and a hole for the inkwell on the upper right, faced east. The east wall of the room was all glass, with the high school library behind, where a teacher could sit and monitor both rooms. Above this glass wall was a picture of the sitting president, Franklin D. Roosevelt, and beside it a picture of the lady who was head of the county education department. Put kindly, the president was not only the prettiest of the two, but the more pleasant looking.

The theory was we would select the classes we wanted. In reality most of the decisions were governed by the fact there were only so many classes available and most being requirements you had a list of one class per period to make your selection from. Algebra was taught one year and Geometry the next, General science one year and Chemistry the next. Ancient History one year and Modern History the next. Those who started the wrong year had a problem. My first year was the year Geometry was taught. Algebra, generally considered the first step wasn't. The next year was Trigonometry. I can't say that I every suffered greatly from it, but I never did get around to taking Algebra.

All science classes were in the room at the south east corner of the building. I remember little of what I was taught in this room. It like all rooms in the school had all walls covered by green colored blackboards. At the rear of the room there were tables with long metal sinks inset into the centers and various pieces of lab equipment sitting on them. Things like beakers in ring stands, pipettes, and Bunsen burners, and one item who's name I can't remember.

They say that when people get old they lose their short term memory. Doesn't this prove I'm not old? I can remember what I did yesterday, but not some people's names or the names of gadgets, of sixty odd years ago. Anyway this one was our favorite gadget when supervision was lax.

This gadget had a clear plastic wheel, probably twenty four inches in diameter, with brushes with long stiff bristles connected to two curved and moveable arms, with steel balls of about one inch diameter on the end. The brushes rubbed on the wheel when it was spun by means of a crank and gears, causing static electricity to build up in the balls, and would make a spark several inches long between the two balls, demonstrating static electricity.

That's how it was supposed to work. It was possible, after carefully moving the two arms together to discharge any electricity, to take hold of one of the arms while someone else turned the crank. The trick was, don't crank too long because it was painful if the charge got high enough to arc across to the other pole of the gadget. The aim was to charge the holdee's body enough that he could walk across to another room and point his finger at some unsuspecting student' ear. The crack of the arcing static charge was always good for an outburst from the receiver, that teachers for some reason seemed to find annoying.

History, Social Studies, and I believe Math were taught in the room on the south west corner of the building. Other than Math, these were never my favorites. Education people considered the subjects important to our life, but I have almost no recollections of anything that transpired in this room, even though several classes were requirements and I must have taken several classes there. Probably all out of date now anyway. What they taught as modern history is now included in ancient history. And reference was made to Einstein's theory and the fact that only a few people in the world understood it.

The English Department lived in the small room in the north west corner of the building, at the back of the study hall. I think it was the same size as the library at the other end. With about twenty chairs, students were crowded up around the teachers desk that was at the center of one side. This desk was the temporary abode of usually very young ladies. I say temporary as they seemed to decide early on that Ione wasn't really the place they were seeking. I will cite a couple of happenings that some might opine had something to do with these decisions.

For one thing, the teachers desk appeared to attract both snakes and frogs. This is surprising as the two are usually not found in the same location, except when the frog is inside the snake. Young English teachers seemed to be surprised to find them in desk drawers, even though usually only one at a time.

About the first of December, a Christmas Tree decorated mostly with candies including gum drops, appeared in one corner of the room, despite the fact the room was so crowded that one or two desks had to be pushed under the tree. This room, as others, had blackboards on both front and back walls. The teacher would be writing on the board at the front behind her desk and would turn around to find the whole class, at least the boys, munching on gum drops. Probably not very nice as she was decorating said tree herself from a very limited income.

The third happening that seemed to disconcert her involved the electric service. As previously noted, the high school was on the third floor. The north side of the English room was three windows wide. The electric service for the school entered through a three inch steel pipe that ran down between windows one and two, and created an easy slide down to the ground. In warm weather the windows would be open, the teacher again at the board with her back to the students. She would turn around and find several of the boys gone from their seats. She knew they hadn't gone out either of the two doors as the doors were within her sight when she was at the board. Appeared to confuse and disconcert her no end.

Some assignments in English involved reading from library books. Naturally the boys were aware of some books or passages in books in the library, I'm not sure why they were there, that were very risqué in those days. Probably used for Sunday school texts today. After getting the teacher to agree that any book from the library was OK, several of the boys chose these for their reading to the class. The room sure got quiet in a hurry.

We always wondered if some of these events could have had something to do with the fact that the English teacher never came back from her Christmas vacation. A series of unrelated pranks, by a group of unthinking kids, that taken all together, may have led to a tragic, unforeseen, result in the life of a very young teacher.

CHAPTER XX

As I mentioned before, many activities other than school took place in the school gym. I don't have too many memories of the Christmas programs, band concerts, various basketball games whether involving mules or Globe Trotters, or most of the plays. It occurs that I may have brought some of it on myself, but I do have memories of a few in which I was personally involved and usually personally embarrassed.

My freshman year, which would have been the fall of 1940, a Halloween dance was held in the gym with refreshments in the basement all purpose room. I allowed someone, with the collusion of my mother, to talk me into going as an old fashioned girl. I was tall and skinny, but after they got me costumed, complete with long dress, poke bonnet, mask, and padding in appropriate places, I seemed to pass muster.

I was never much into dancing, which a boy can get away with, but was unheard of in girls. Besides I really wasn't interested in dancing with any of the boys. There must have been at least one of the guys at the dance who didn't try to dance with the strange new girl, but at the time I would have argued the point. I finally slipped out the back door to get away and that turned out to be a strategic error also. I'm not sure what they were doing out there, probably grabbing a smoke, but there were a bunch of boys out behind the gym and I was no longer protected by the bright lights and chaperones. It didn't occur to me at the time, but a dress might be a good incentive for inspiring the track team. I'm not sure if any of the track team were represented in the group, but I managed to outdistance them all. I never did get back to the dance for any of the promised refreshments.

Another instance involved my old nemesis, the eighth grade teacher, principal. The school, probably under the auspices of the English Department, put on it's annual play, This year the Pirates of Penzance was chosen. I was one of the chorus line. All I can remember of one of the songs we were to sing is, "We were once as band of pirates, brave and bold, patterned after men who lived in stories old." We were dressed in stagged off jeans, ragged sweat shirts, and someone's idea of pirate hats, and told to move and act like a happy bunch of swaggering pirates.

Midway through the song I looked down the line and found all of the other guys were standing like wooden Indians, so I gave up and joined them. The next day, the man, who was my shop teacher, jumped me in front of a bunch of the guys and dressed me down for smarting off and ruining the play for everybody. He didn't have his paddle along, but I knew better than to dispute him by pointing out I was the only one doing as told, as there were lots of sticks laying around handy in the woodshop.

I'm not sure what year it was, but one trip from high school days was the time we went to Z Canyon. It couldn't happen today because everyone is too concerned about liability. I'm afraid I did mostly watch, so guess there wasn't so much liability involved in my case, but I do remember the two logs laid across the canyon with board cleats nailed on top. I have seen photos from earlier times of people on a proper bridge spanning the canyon, but it wasn't in place when we were up there. I think it was only seventeen feet across the river. The saying was, the river turned on it's side to get through the canyon. Some of the guys must have been much braver than I as they actually crawled across, but not me.

Then we went to Gardener Cave. At that time it was just a hole in the ground. Someone had cut the limbs off a tree, leaving stubs sticking out about six inches, and stood it in the hole. We crawled down the ladder/tree, to a level about fifteen feet down. From there it was necessary to lay down and slide through a narrow opening to continue. I don't think we had any lights, and they tell me it was very dark. I'll never know. Guess I wasn't very brave.

It's not connected to any thing, but I just remembered something involving Deans Grocery and Mercantile at the corner of Main and The Highway where the Mountain Trader is now located. There were three groceries in the town at that time and Deans was the first to disappear, early in the 1930's when the mill departed. At the time, it was against the law to sell margarine in Washington State as a result of the farm lobby protecting their own. It had to be special ordered from out of state by a specific consumer. At the time, it sold for about ten cents a pound and we were able to sell our butter for about twenty five so we sold butter and ate margarine. Deans cheated a bit. They kept the margarine hidden in the cooler and when we went in we bought from it and signed an order with which they could replenish their supply later. Don't worry Deans. I'm sure the law is no longer looking for you.

Later, this law was repealed or modified until it was still not legal to sell colored margarine, but legal to sell it white. I can remember sitting and coloring it because everybody thought it didn't taste the same when white. At first it came in a paper carton with an envelope of an orange colored powder that had to be mixed in with a fork and took a long time. Later it came in a tough plastic bag with a color capsule inside. It was necessary to pop the plastic capsule and then knead the bag until the color was evenly mixed. It still took a long time.

After Deans closed as a grocery, the building became a de facto mattress factory. This was one of the Roosevelt era things to help recovery from the depression. Both the farmers and the end receivers would benefit. Blue gray striped ticking that looked like it was for prison uniforms, probably surplus from somewhere, and surplus cotton bats were furnished. The people were able to make their own mattresses, usually to replace ticks make of burlap bags sewn together and stuffed with straw.

My mother was one of those who helped teach the people how. The ticking was cut and sewn into mattress shape and laid out on two mattress sized low tables. Next thin layers of cotton batting were laid inside of it. As each layer was added the bats were beaten with thin bamboo sticks about four feet long so the cotton bonded together, then another layer was added and it was again beaten. We kids spent a lot of time wielding the sticks. It was a lot more fun at the beginning than it got to be later. And we slept on a couple of the resulting mattresses until we left Ione.

CHAPTER XXI

By the 1940-41 school year the war had begun to loom and we began to lose students again. I was too young to be effected directly, but all boys over eighteen were required to register for the draft. Any with less than six months of high school to go, and I think it applied to college also, were allowed a deferment to finish school. Some locals were drafted, and a few more enlisted in other branches to avoid being drafted into the Army.

I believe this may have effected my life indirectly in that I ended up with almost more jobs than I wanted. I think it was Gerald McFall, who's dad was postmaster, who worked for Hansens Bakery. He said he was going to quit in the spring, I'm not sure if for the service or for college. I applied, and got the job. The bakery was located where the lumber yard for the present Country Hardware store is today.

I was required to be at the store by six in the morning, which severely limited any desire for any night life. My first duty of the day was to flag the oven. The oven was a room size red brick structure, with an interior opening approximately two feet high and probably eight feet square, and a door on front about a foot high and two feet wide with a pair of steel doors to close it.

Four foot lengths, of cord wood, were loaded in at night and burned inside the oven overnight. By the next morning they were reduced to a few ashes which

I would clean out by means of a "flag." The, "flag," was a burlap sack on the end of a pole, just a small sapling, about ten feet long. The sack was soaked in a pail of water to somewhat fireproof it and set to spinning on the end of the pole, inside the oven. The ashes were all swept out to the opening by the spinning burlap bag, to where they could be swept up. This was expected to take me less than half an hour.

It was essential the oven be loaded and fired again at the end of each day, so it still had enough heat to cause a draft to start the wood burning, so it was fired even on Sunday although the store wasn't open.

Mr. Hansen was always there and working when I arrived, and would have been making bread dough and forming it into loaves. As soon as the oven was cleaned he would insert the pans into the oven, by setting them on the end of a long handled paddle like is used in a pizza oven. By the time the bread was baked the oven would be cooled enough that bread rolls and cinnamon rolls went in, followed by smaller rolls, cookies, and cake doughnuts as it cooled further. It was all choreographed so we would prepare each item as the oven cooled to the temperature needed to bake it.

I would fry glazed doughnuts and maple bars and help with the rolls at the same time. I would work until I barely had time to make deliveries of doughnuts and rolls to the restaurants and still make the bell at school less than two blocks away.

Two memories both involve square five gallon cans. Cashew nuts came in the cans, at what I thought a terrible price. The can said they came from India and Mr. Hansen said the can cost, I think twelve dollars, probably somewhere around fifty cents a pound. He saw me nibbling on one and urged me to eat all I wanted. Actually he did the same with pastries. I found out why when after a couple of days I couldn't stand the sight of either of them.

The other memory was the same can, after it had been emptied of nuts. Each morning I would break about a dozen eggs into the can, on top of those remaining from before, and stir them up. They became rather ripe after a few days but we didn't worry about it or ever throw any of them away. They were used to paint the tops of the various rolls to give them that nice shiny brown top, and he said they worked better after they had aged a few days.

At lunch time I would return to the bakery and make deliveries to the three stores and several restaurants around town at the time. We had a wooden push cart with two bicycle wheels that would hold enough bread and rolls to cover most of the town if I figured right and there hadn't been some unusual rush on them. I don't remember the price of rolls, but I think bread was ten cents a loaf wholesale for the full loaf. There was also a short loaf, about two thirds as big, of which I don't remember the price. The stores would sell the big loaf for fifteen cents and the small for ten cents, I think.

I think it was in the fall of that year that I picked up the third job. I still had the janitor job at the school in the evenings. The Ione Theater was on the corner of Main Street and the highway, where the Baptist Church is today It was operated by George Widger, who ran the Power and Light office, and his wife Nina who was a telephone operator across the street, as ticket seller.

The projectionist was a man named Johnson, who was a local electrician who possibly worked for Widger at the power company. I was hired to be his assistant. It was never sure why two people were necessary, until much later when it dawned on me that it might have been because of his fondness for demon rum, that my position was necessary. Most of the operating time was spent sitting in the booth that was even hot in winter and peering at the screen through a tiny window. After a few hours, and a few times with the same show, a person might fall asleep. Especially if under the right stimuli.

The booth was located up in the rear of the theater, above the lobby, and was reached by scaling a ladder up through a trapdoor. The two 35mm projectors, probably modified from the old silent movie days, were not matched and were far from reliable. I think the reason Mr. Johnson. kept the job was because he was the only one who could keep them running. We were at the end of the film distribution chain so the films came in scratched and with numerous splices, so interruptions of the show weren't unusual.

The projectors were Simplex, and ran fairly well, even if noisy. The light sources fitted to them were Standards that burned carbon rods to produce a very bright white light. It was also a very hot light and in those days, film was nitrate base, somewhere west of gunpowder in volatility.

The operator would set the carbons in the lights, load a reel of film on each machine, start the first one, divide his attention between the projector and the light, and also watch the picture for focus, through his little window. The carbons were advanced as they burned by electric motors that were supposed to keep them set right, and usually did fairly well. If the gap got too wide the light would go out. If too narrow the light would slowly get dimmer and redder.

The idea was to watch the machine until it got

close to the end of the reel, then watch through the little window and catch the change-over cue on the screen. At the first cue the second machine was started, and ten seconds later on the second cue you hit the dowser that dropped down in front of the first machine at the same time it opened up the second one. This was the time, while you were totally preoccupied, that the carbons would usually chose to get out of sync. Many films were black and white yet, but color was coming. The only one I can recall was a color film, something like "Dawn Patrol," a WW1 airplane film, with old biplanes flitting around on bright blue skies, shooting at each other. Of course the good guys always came out on top.

One show that I do recall, I can't even remember the picture's name. I was watching through my little window, probably at least half awake, when I noticed some odd effects. I sat wondering how they got those effects in the movie for several seconds before it dawned on me that I was doing it. The film had broken and was feeding down into the gate at about three feet per second, where it stopped so it was burning up and the image of the smoke was being projected onto the screen.

It was an interesting effect, but my next question was, will it go out or will it climb up the film and set off the whole reel if I shut it off. The people watching the films were always so supportive when things like this happened and it would be necessary to shut down and reload. We probably also heard from the viewers the next day when the film was next run, minus the several seconds of film that had burned.

CHAPTER XXII

The high school enrollment continued to decline into the forties. Our Freshman class in the spring of 1941 had shrunk to fifteen students. The Sophmore class photo in the spring of 1942 had only twelve. The loss of three doesn't sound like many, but with the small class that was twenty percent. Again I'm not sure how many went into the military and how many just moved out with families looking to find employment elsewhere. The need for metals for war production increased so the mines were going great, but the workers in the mines were younger and their kids likewise, so the grade school population actually went up.

We were hearing reports of atrocities committed by the Japanese in China and also by the Nazis in Europe, but there was much disagreement about whether they were the truth or not, and whether we should be concerned. President Roosevelt was a hero to most people because of his actions to alleviate the effects of the depression and was elected to unprecedented third and fourth terms, but this approval wasn't universal.

General McAthur ran against him the last time because the faction he represented wanted us to enter the war and considered Roosevelt too soft. Others, conversely, opposed him as being a warmonger. He was in favor of out helping the English. To some this was all a Jewish plot and they referred to him as

President Rosenfelt. I don't think most of us kids, other than those looking to be drafted, were even aware of most of this.

Some influential people including everyone's hero, Charles Lindberg, and some of the Kennedys, were in favor of our aiding Germany because they were sure the German Armies would come out on top and it would be to our advantage to be on the winning team after the war.

Many of the young guys enlisted in various branches of the service, but a lot of men looked for ways to dodge the service by getting jobs offering deferrals. Various dissimilar jobs like farming and working in war plants qualified. These men were looked down on by most as draft dodgers. There was no running off to Canada then as Canada was already in the war.

Blocked by congress in his attempt to help The English financially, President Roosevelt came up with, "Lend Lease." He "lent," them forty old worn out destroyers and some were in favor of impeaching him for doing this. Mostly the destroyers were used to convoy ships, most of them ours, through the German U-Boats of the North Atlantic. Most of these were carrying war materials to England and later, many to Russia, again mostly on lend lease. But the companies producing the stuff being shipped were only too happy for the business after the depression, so it was for the most part kept under the radar. Or would have been if radar had been invented at least.

All of this changed after Pearl Harbor. The attack happened on Sunday morning, but I think most of us learned about it at school on Monday. There was much talk about the, "little yellow devils," and their cowardly attack and how we would smash them as soon as our men could catch up with them.

This war propaganda, that was told as fact at the time, went on everywhere you went. Posters warning against fifth columnists. The famous recruiting poster of Uncle Sam pointing and saying, "I Want You." "Loose Lips Sink Ships," and many others. I'm sure the flag waving accelerated the enlistments into the various services as it was meant to do.

I imagine it looked different from their side, but I was never aware of any threats or adverse comments against the Terroka family, who operated the Ione Steam Laundry located next to the bank on Main Street. Grace was in my class. I never got along too well with her but that had nothing to do with the war. Mary was about two years younger and once parted my hair with a two by four, but that again was a kid thing and several years before the war. Pauline was a couple years older and was always my buddy.

Many people in Metaline Falls sent their laundry out of town because of the cement plant. Laundry hung out to dry, this was before dryers, came in stiff as a board from cement dust in the air. One has to wonder what it did to lungs, but I don't recall anyone being concerned at the time. Much of the laundry came to Ione and Terroka's laundry. I rode with Pauline many times on trips to pick up the dirty and deliver the clean.

Harold Matsuda would have probably been the first suspect as the latest arrival from Japan, and because he was of military age, but again I do not remember any but good feeling toward him. I have heard since that the people in Metaline Falls barricaded the bridge over the river and wouldn't let the Feds take their only Japanese, the Kubota family who ran the local hardware and were big in civic affairs of the town, when they started relocating people to the internment centers away from most anything that could be called a war related zone.

I'm not sure if it was the spring or the fall term of 1942 that the great scrap metal drive took place. The high school chose up sides, freshmen and seniors against the sophomores and juniors and scoured the countryside for miles around for any metal laying around. One side built a pile in the backstop of the baseball diamond west of the school and the other piled theirs out behind second base.

I'm not sure what ever became of the scrap or which side won the contest. The railroad had long since ceased operation and I'm not sure how many trucks would be needed and if it would be worth the shipping to take the scrap to the nearest railhead.

I don't remember how many trucks were used in the gathering, very few of the students had cars to drive to school at the time, but do I remember an incident with an old Chev flatbed that ran when ever it took a notion. There were six or eight of us involved when the truck stalled on the rise by the cemetery. Elmer Skjeie, (pronounced Shay) and I, long time buddies, had been cutting up, pushing each other back and forth throughout the trip. I was standing, watching someone work under the truck hood, holding on to the door post of the open drivers side door with my right hand. He ran past my back and slugged me and slammed the truck door.

I stood with my right index finger in the hinge side of the closed door and couldn't reach the handle to open it. I yelled, but he wouldn't come back and let me loose as he thought I was just trying to catch him. It's now over sixty years later and I still have an index finger that's flat on the end and a nail that grows weird.

It was just before Christmas in 1942 when we joined the exodus. My folks heard from my grandparents that there was plenty of work in the shipyards in the Portland area. Actually the companies were shipping people in from all over the country. Ole took off first and when he had saved enough for the fare we joined him.

Pay was high by the standards we were used to, but by today's doesn't sound so good. In most trades, journeyman could be reached in three to six months. A journeyman welder or ship fitter earned $71.76 for a forty eight hour week, or $1.38 per hour for straight time. I was pleasantly surprised a couple months after we left, when the student body took up a collection and sent me a going away present of a sweater.

In March of the next year, someone waved a flag at me and I went into the Army Air Corps. The only trip I ever made back to Ione was after the war in about 1947 when the family, all six of us, piled into the family thirty seven Chev sedan and drove up. Actually we came mostly to visit Ole's mother in Kettle Falls and I only spent one day back in Ione.

I remember few details of the trip other than: How good the iced watermelon was at the stand outside of Hermiston in the heat of the Saturday afternoon. Dropping a valve keeper on an overhead valve of the car, just south of Spokane, about daylight on Sunday morning, and limping into town with it rattling on the top of the piston. A kindly and sympathetic mechanic, hand made a replacement for next to nothing and got us back on the road. Times were definitely different.

The third was to find the Hotel Pend Oreille in Ione, that we had played in as kids, open for business.

We stopped for breakfast at the restaurant. The Picnik family had opened the restaurant, and I believe they had redone and were renting some of the second floor rooms.

My next visit wasn't until about fifty years later.